WINE MADE EASY

GIANLUCA ROTTURA

Owner of
IN VINO VERITAS

Copyright © 2004 (Original Paperback)
Copyright © 2019 (Updated, Second Edition Paperback)

All rights reserved. Printed in the United States of America. No part of this publication may be reproduced, stored in a retrieval system, or transmitted, in any form or by any means electronic, mechanical, photocopying, recording, or otherwise, without the prior written permission of the author.

ISBN 978-0-578-59161-2

CONTENTS

Acknowledgements 4
Introduction 5
How Wine Is Made 8
New World Wines 12
Critics 15
Tasting Wine 16
General Wine Terms 20
Serving and Storing Wine 28
Argentina 30
Australia 32
Austria 34
California 36
Chile 40
Croatia 41
Czech Republic 42
France 43
Georgia 57
Germany 58
Greece 63
Hungary 67
Israel 69
Italy 72
Lebanon 101
Morocco 102
New York 103
New Zealand 104
Oregon 106
Portugal 108
Slovenia 112
South Africa 113
Spain 114
Switzerland 119
Turkey 121
Uruguay 122
Washington 106
Matching Wine With Food 123
Menu With Matching Wines 124
Retail 136
Restaurants 138
Index 139

ACKNOWLEDGEMENTS

First and Foremost, I would like to thank all my customers
for their trust and continued support.

Next, I would like to thank all of those who have brought us so many great wines.

Third, I would like to thank my family; the store wouldn't be possible without my Parents, Alberto and Liliana. To my Grandparents, Aunts, Uncles, and Cousins who all made and make wine, thanks for inspiring me. I give eternal thanks to my Wife, Barbara, and Children, Alessia and Francesca, because that's what Life is all about. Extra special thanks to my Brother, Gianbruno, for being the one to craft and curate one of the World's best wine selections. Of course, my great wine staff, throughout the many years, deserves a thank you for all they have done. Shoutouts to Evan, Irbing, Kevin, Ken, and all the many others who we helped us along the way. My friends who supported me get all my Love. John Mark, my best friend and biggest supporter (in Life and in wine book sales), I Love you. Keep watching over us. And, for Chip, my I.T. guy, who saved me from going crazy dealing with technology.

Extra Special Thanks to:

All the teachers who told me I was wrong, stupid, and hopeless.
To the teachers who held my head down on my desk and smashed it with their palms.
For all the times I was thrown out of the classrooms just for disagreeing.
Passing off the required low grades to me to help fill your quotas.
To every other person who doubted me.

P.S. I wrote a book to make you look.

INTRODUCTION

In this day and age, anyone can write a book on anything. Go to a bookstore and have yourself a laugh. There are books ranging from "How To Match Your Socks and Tupper Ware" to "How To Sue Companies That Make You Fat." The books written on wine are more than numerous. Some are fantastic and very informative. Others are average, but, hey, what can you do? Wine is a very hard topic to cover. That is why I decided to summarize everything. More importantly, I added a little advice here and there. The advice you may ignore, if you wish, but the rest are good facts you should know.

While writing this book, a friend asked, "Well, what makes you qualified to write a book?" I was surprised he would ask me that. I thought he would put 2 and 2 together. He is a friend and does know who I am but, you, the reader, probably do not. So, it is only fair that you ask, "Hey buddy, what makes you qualified to write a wine book, heh?"

I was born and raised in New York City to Italian immigrants. I was raised in a very old-fashioned household and the Italian culture played a big role in my life. I drank wine when I was just a toddler and remember telling my elementary school teachers that I drank it at dinner. They lost their minds, demanding to know, "What do you mean wine at dinner? You're only six!" I responded, "Look. Relax. It's better than a cup of milk. And, besides, peanut butter sandwiches are not considered dinner at my house." Dinner at my house was a feast. I was not like the other kids. I loved eating all kinds of vegetables. I ate things that are now considered delicacies that would make a kid, and some adults, throw up. At an early age, I was pairing wine with food. It was just a natural thing for me. When I went to Italy every summer, I watched my relatives work in the vineyards.

Back home, in Manhattan, New York City, my father had a very successful, Italian restaurant, Sistina. I learned the business, which is not as glamorous as most people think. By age 18, my brother and I were running our family's own wine shop, In Vino Veritas. Our shop is truly a New York City Landmark; it is believed to be the first liquor store to open in Manhattan after Prohibition ended. My family took it over in April 1997 and dedicated a full year to completely renovating the store. What was once an old, shabby, typical, liquor store had been turned into a jewel of a wine shop.

There were maybe only a handful of "nice-looking" stores in New York City and probably fewer across the country when we first got started. One glance at In Vino Veritas is like a glimpse into an era past. The museum look of the shop is one of a kind. Unearthed during the renovation process were huge pieces of stained glass dating back to the 1800's. The prized glass was restored to its former glory and we inserted the new store name into it. It's almost impossible anymore to find that much antique, stained glass outside of Churches. The inside is enchanting as it is welcoming. Everything from the Murano lamps to the original brick wall that had been exposed are all signs of the passion and reverence my family has for Beauty. We believe that In Vino Veritas was on the forefront of helping change wine store looks, layouts, and wine selections in New York City, and, given everyone takes note of what happens in the Big Apple, this echoed across the country and eventually the World.

What is perhaps a true sign of passion is the climate-controlled wine cellar, where every bottle of wine sold to the customer is kept at a perfect temperature. The most exciting part of In Vino Veritas is the carefully hand-picked wine selection. My brother, Gianbruno, and I tasted thousands of wines and began learning more than ever. We went to almost every tasting there was, read a lot of books, and picked the brains of the World's best winemakers.

At our store, we make our wine selection by carefully choosing wines and drinking them with a specifically tailored dinner our mother makes. If we are trying a new Montepulciano, you can bet we are probably having a plate of Bucatini all' Amatriciana with it. Having owned a world famous and prestigious Italian restaurant in the past and having farms and vineyards back in Italy, my family is very aware of the importance of wine and food matching. Most restaurants and retail stores rarely try the wines they sell and, if and when they do, they almost never would make the wine selection based on how it pairs it with food. At our store, we always ask customers if they are eating and, if so, what food(s).

We at In Vino Veritas have a different approach from many others; we go out of our way to not only befriend the owners of the wineries that make the wines we sell but have dinner with them, too, whether in New York City or at their wineries around the World. To go the extra length, we feel confident in our selection because, in a city where a new wine distributor pops up every day with a portfolio of new wines to try, we are under attack from many bad products. Any sommelier at a fancy restaurant can make a good to great wine list when they are only presented the best but try finding a real wine that represents that grape's and location's character for 10 bucks wholesale. Good luck, because, besides a few stores like ours, you won't find any. My brother and I went out of our ways to try it all, from the worst wines to the very best. We love to specialize in inexpensive gems precisely because they are harder and harder to find.

In Vino Veritas also offers free wine tastings that allow people to taste wines they might otherwise never have thought of trying. Teaching about wine is very important to us. In fact, I spent over two decades as a wine educator, lecturer, and even newspaper writer. The newspaper articles were for a media company that didn't really have its act together and ruined quite a few of my pieces. They were in the beginning stages and their inexperience showed. Now, they are huge and most of my articles are washed away online, but I managed to save each print version of each article. The wine education is key, which is where this book comes in.

I always wanted to write my own book, but never got around to it. On the evening of December 14, 2002, I started writing. I realized how hard it was to write a book. I had so many ideas that I did not know where to start. Somehow, just four weeks later, during the busy Christmas season, I finished. I could not believe it. The long and arduous process of publishing is what I found ahead of me.

Like everything in Life, there were numerous obstacles to get to where I now find myself. I already have had four sinus operations. I have a hard time breathing and smelling. It is better now, but not 100%. Sometimes I can smell anything. Other times, I can't even smell garlic. I guess this obstacle really pushed me to write a book on something I love but cannot always fully appreciate.

N.B. I updated and re-published this book. The "long and arduous process of publishing is what I found ahead of me" happened again. And 3 sinus operations became 4. When I first wrote the book in 2002, I only mentioned wines that were available in the States. Since then, thankfully, many more different types of wonderful wines have reached our shores and, so, I added them in this book.

HOW WINE IS MADE

This alone can be a thousand-page book in itself. Winemaking is an extremely lengthy and arduous process. I can only speak of it in general terms. There are two places involved in winemaking: **the vineyard and the winery.**

IN THE VINEYARD

Many wine makers always say, "Wine is made first and foremost in the vineyard." This is, in a sense, very true. If you have bad grapes, you are probably going to have bad wine. On the other hand, if you have good grapes, it will be easier to make good wine. There are many crucial components that determine everything in the vineyard.

The main ones are: *Location, Weather, Vines, Grapes.*

Location

My father always told me how his father's wines always tasted different than his uncle's, even though their vineyards touched. Differences in wine can be greatly varied, even from grapes grown in neighboring vineyards. The ideal location for a vineyard is on a slope. Slopes get the most sunlight. It is as simple as that. Altitude is also important but varies greatly depending on which grapes are being grown. Riesling and Sauvignon Blanc do well at high altitudes, while Zinfandel and Shiraz do well at lower altitudes, for example. Some vineyards are situated next to rivers, which are ideal, because they act as heat storage places for grapes. Other vineyards, like those in Rhône, have stones on top of the soil, which also capture and trap heat. The soil must be well drained in order to provide the vines with an optimum supply of water and nutrients.

Weather

Each vineyard has its own climate, better known as microclimates. To be even more specific, each vine has its own microclimate. Each of these microclimates heavily influences the vines and, therefore, the grapes. Again, certain grapes do better in cool climates, while others prefer hotter climates.

Vines

Good vines make good wine, right? Pretty much, but it is not that easy. When vines are young (under 25 years), they produce a lot of grapes and in turn a lot of wine. This is a winemaker's gift from God. Plentiful crops help pay the bills plus pay for momma's brand-new bag. As vines get older, (35 years+) they begin to produce less grapes, but of much higher quality. These vines are usually called "old vines" or in French "vielles vignes". Too many winemakers rip out older vines for the guaranteed cash crops. Younger vines produce more and that is usually the winery's goal. Though older vines produce better, more expensive wines, "Old Vines" on a label does not always guarantee quality. Some wineries make bad wine from old vines and still charge too much money. Vines also have their share of hard times. They have to fight off various fungal and bacterial infections, including extreme weather conditions. On top of that, they have to duke it out with every insect on the planet. A very important practice called Pruning helps maintain the vines to assure a high-quality, yielding crop. Pruning is when a wine maker clips away some fruit to keep the vines from over producing. This practice strengthens the vines and, most importantly, greatly improves the quality of the grapes. Pruning also makes harvesting a much easier process, giving you better grapes with concentrated flavors and fewer flaws.

Grapes

Picking the grapes at the right time is one of the trickiest things for a wine maker. They have to time it just right where the sugars and acidity are at their correct levels. Small, quick changes in weather can screw everything up. Harvesting may be done mechanically or by hand. The harvest is very decisive in determining with what you will end up.

IN THE WINERY

Here is where man (or woman) can perfect or ruin everything. It is all left to the winemaker to not only express his desire for the wine style but to take advantage of that current harvest's positives and downplay, even eliminate, any possible negatives.
General Steps to making Wine:

Red Wine
The grapes are either completely or partially destemmed.

Then, the red grapes are crushed.

The juice is left to ferment with the skins and sometimes even the stems.

The winemaker at this point may enact Chaptalization or Acidification,
only if the law of the country allows it.

Chaptalization is adding extra sugar if there is little in the must.

Acidification is the addition of extra acidity if there is little in the must.

The juice may be further kept in contact with the skins and stems
for extra color, flavor, and tannins.

The wine is then either transferred to
wood barrels, usually oak, or stainless steel vats for ageing.

The wine at this point may undergo a second fermentation,
more commonly referred to as Malolactic Fermentation.

This converts the sharp tasting malic acid into lactic acid, which is softer.

All wines from all barrels or stainless steel vats are tasted and may be blended with other wines made from different grapes. White wine is sometimes blended into red. The wine may or may not undergo a filtration process to remove unwanted impurities.

The wine is bottled and may remain at the winery for further ageing, taking place in the bottle itself.

White Wine

The grapes are destemmed and crushed.

The juice from white grapes rarely ever stays in contact with the skins.

The juice is fermented, at this point, you can do Chaptalization or Acidification.

The wine is then transferred to wood barrels or stainless steel vats.

The wine may undergo malolactic fermentation. This process is fine for red wines but can make whites taste boring and milk-like.

The wine may be blended with juice from other white grapes.

The wine is bottled.

Rosé Wine

Rosé wines can be made in 2 ways:

1) By fermenting the juice of red grapes with the skins for only a short period of time. Once the desired color is obtained, the skins are separated from the juice.

2) By blending white wine with red wine. This practice is illegal in Europe, except in the French region of Champagne.

The wines may undergo malolactic fermentation.

The wines may be aged in oak barrels or stainless steel vats.

The wine is bottled.

Orange Wine
Orange wine is made with white grapes. Once pressed, the skins, pulp, and seeds are left in contact with the juice much longer than they would if just white wine were being made. The resulting wine has an orange color to it and the flavors are much deeper and bolder. Orange wines can be honeyed and nutty, with flavors of dried fruit and somewhat oxidized, in a good way.

Sweet Wine
Sweet wines can be made in 2 ways:
1) By stopping the fermentation early. At this point, not all the sugar has been converted to alcohol. The remaining sugar is called residual sugar.
2) The must is so high in sugar, that the fermentation may stop by itself leaving a lot of the sugar not converted to alcohol.
The sweet wine may be aged in oak barrels or stainless steel.
The wine is bottled.

Sparkling Wine
During fermentation, the yeasts convert the grapes' sugars into alcohol and carbon dioxide is released. To make sparkling wines, you trap the carbon dioxide and bubbles are formed. Sparkling wine can be made in many ways but the 3 most important are the **Traditional Method** (Méthode Traditionelle), **Charmat-Martinotti** (Tank Method), and **Pétillant Naturel** (Méthode Ancestrale).

The Traditional Method, also called Méthode Champenoise only in the region of Champagne, is when the secondary fermentation takes place in the bottle itself. In the Charmat-Martinotti method, the secondary fermentation takes place in a tank. Pétillant-Naturel (A.K.A. Pét-Nat) is the oldest form of sparkling wine, where the wine is removed from the vat midway during fermentation and continues its one fermentation (not two fermentations like the others) in the bottle itself. The resulting wine can be cloudy, funky, and a little sweeter and less bubbly than the more common sparkling wines.

NEW WORLD WINES

The term New World wines refers to all the countries that are pretty new to the wine game. These New World countries (U.S.A., Chile, Argentina, Uruguay, New Zealand, Australia, and South Africa) borrowed the grapes from Europe and attempted to model their wines after those from France and Italy. The resulting wines are by no means similar to those from Europe. New World wine countries consistently follow trends without failure. Trends, however, do not necessarily coincide with quality. California is THE symbol and leading representative of the New World wine countries. I have tasted some amazing New World wines, most hailing from California. I have also tasted a lot of crap, mostly from California.

How did New World wines get so popular? I do not know. The typical answer is that producers did this and that, experimented with cutting edge whatever, and a whole bunch of other boring stuff. In the U.S.A., California is known as "The Wine Country." What does that mean? Whole countries like France, Italy, and Spain are wine countries in their entirety. My answer : California wines achieved success because the "Wine Country" is a wine business, not a wine producer. I have no problems with big business. In fact, I have no problem with California wine companies. I have a problem with the fact that people have to pay obscene prices for ordinary crap, while real deal, passionate California winemakers get overlooked and even pushed to the side. Actually, let me replace the words "have to pay" with "willing to pay". That's right; the problem is the consumer. The big, California wine corporations will give the consumer what they want. Educate yourself as a consumer and then demand better. Ask and you will receive. Believe me, your dollars will not be denied.

Big, California wine corporations spend tons of money to try to get you to drink their wine. The wine-shy consumer is so afraid of wine that they run to the name they have heard over and over again. They think they are playing it safe but, in reality, they are playing it wrong. Chances are, if you buy a mass-produced, California wine, you are getting something that is more of a concoction than wine. Phrases like "aged for a refined flavor" are misleading. Instead, wood chips and, sometimes, even powder essences are stirred in to add flavor. Too often, this process is so overwhelmingly evident, it tastes as if they put wine in a bucket of wood chips.

New World wineries also unfortunately pride themselves with making 100% of the wine strictly from one grape. They rarely blend; blending can enhance certain positive characteristics, may soften the wine's rough character, or can even bulk up a boring wine. With too many New World wines, you are usually getting 100% Cabernet or Merlot (which is generally useless by itself) and this is the case with many other grape varieties, too. The problem is you are getting all the Cabernet and Merlot that is available and that includes the *possible* negative aspects of how those grapes came out. On top of that, you are getting the exaggerated expressions of the grape.

More is not necessarily better and large, New World, New Style wineries don't get that. The most important aspect of a good wine is balance. Too many New World wines have their components all over the place. The over ripe, too-bold fruit is one place, while the acidity (whatever little exists) is far off, nowhere to be found.

Unfortunately, some Europeans are abandoning old, tried and proven styles to produce "New Style" wines and shooting themselves in the foot and increasingly losing credibility among true wine lovers. The New World obsession with super fruity, oaky wines with no acidity or character has been morphing into a global movement. It seems as if there were a forced and orchestrated push to view winemaking like a pyramid. All the grapes of the world are on the bottom. There are too many, so it's "economical" to do away with most and only focus on the tried and true. Then, the goal is to take all these different and separate grapes on the bottom and make wines that all resemble the one style and flavor profile of the wine at the top. It's as if the winemakers all have horse blinders on, racing to the same goal as everyone else. Done this way, wines no longer have unique character and could never speak of their terroir or their stories. It's foolish and disgusting.

Consumers got mad and now buy less. As with most New World wines, if you had one, you had them all. Why drink the same crap every night? Also, why drink the same crap at such high prices? You might think, "Why is this guy so extreme?" I am not and neither are the thousands of customers who give the New World wine industry a deserved cold shoulder. I have my views; they are not extreme just because you might not happen to agree with them.

California has been waking up. They went through a period where they had representatives go from store to store, restaurant to restaurant. I saw them regularly. They had me blind taste some California wines and then asked me how much I think it was worth and how much the selling price should have been. My estimated worth was always at least half of the asking price. If I said a certain wine was worth $20, it sold for $45. I did not know whether to laugh or cry.

I would estimate that only less than half of all California wine is actually worth buying, when considering price and quality. Unfortunately, eight out of ten good to great California wines are not cheap, due to their brutal, business environment. There is great California wine out there, but the customer must do their homework. I do not mean to bash California wines. I JUST WANT TO PROTECT THE CONSUMER. *In fact, I would love to see the whole world drink California wines and make California rich! The state has the potential and can easily do it.* Search out artisanal, California wine producers and spend your money on their products. You will be satisfied and giving back to the backbone of our great Country.

While California makes great reds, the whites are never my style. If you wish to discover more classy, New World wines, direct your attention to New Zealand, specifically this country's whites. They are still primarily fruit-driven, however, they are much better balanced and more food friendly than most others. Oregon is a great place for Pinot Noir and does not generally overdo their wines.

UPDATE

My criticism of New World Wines in general and California in particular may sound too harsh but, please, take into account that this book was originally written in 2002, when things were indeed that bad! To be fair, many California producers have learned to show more restraint and make more balanced wines now. To go further, the national attention towards organic, farming practices has put the spotlight on California and its organic and sustainable agriculture.

California happens to follow the rules more closely than modern European countries. As I sadly predicted with food, culture, and pretty much everything else, Europe is becoming like the America they ridiculed and America is becoming more like the Europe that is fading away. Again, please know that my disappointment with a chunk of California wines doesn't take away the fact that the state and its people are among the best in the country.

I LOVE California and wish it to succeed!

CRITICS

When you point the finger at someone, there are three pointing back at you. People's ignorance of wine, and food, has allowed a host of jobs to pop up. You have magazines, TV shows, classes, you name it. People's fear of wine has given tremendous power to certain people, sometimes the wrong people. *Some people are so scared of living, they would not even pass gas without first consulting a magazine.* Big magazines have so many wine judges who are told not to give certain wines a bad score. Can you guess why? Well, think about it. If my winery gives your magazine $500,000 a year for advertising, would you have the guts to give my wine a bad score? Add to that a few hundred wineries and you have a rich magazine scared to tell the truth about so many wines.

Then, there are newsletters authored by an individual taster. This is somewhat fair. You can get to know the person's tastes by reading his/her opinions. Either you agree or you do not. The only problem is that some of these writers are so famous and powerful, that their word is believed to be law. Winemakers will change their whole style of wine making just to please the taster and receive high scores. These scores can really make or break a winemaker. Most tasters are very dedicated and love wine. They know so much about wine but still never get it. My point is that *enthusiasm does not necessarily qualify you.*

Do not get me wrong; there are some real good critics out there. The only problem is that these people are a minority and rarely noticed. In this book, I give countless descriptions of many different wines. I felt like an idiot writing the word "cherry" over and over again. The fact is most red wines do have hints of cherry. You can read all the descriptions you want about wine, but it will mean nothing until you try it. *Who knows? You might know more than the critic. It does happen, by the way!* The best story is when a journalist from a very important wine publication (no name) did not know that Sangiovese was an Italian grape. He actually thought it was Californian. These are some of the idiots in charge of judging people's hard work and, to make matters worse, they are getting paid. It is unbelievable.

UPDATE:

In the age of social media "influencers", where mostly not so bright people pose almost naked with a product, did I not hit the nail on the head? Sadly, things have gotten worse and crazier since this original chapter (sans update) was written in 2002. It's now 2019 as I write this and I don't see an end to this madness.

TASTING WINE

I must begin first by saying that you should drink what you like. If you think it is good, then drink up. Apart from specific likes and dislikes, every one of us has a certain preference or tolerance for various degrees of richness, lightness, sweetness, bitterness, acidity, and tannins. Remember: One person's trash is another's treasure. You should know what you like and _why_ you like it. There is no real correct way to judge what is good or bad; however, there are certain steps one should follow when tasting wine.

You may start by pouring roughly 2 ounces into a wine glass of at least 12-ounce capacity. The extra space is crucial for swirling. Swirling is a process that opens up the wine's aromas and releases its flavors. Swirling may seem difficult, but practice will make perfect. For starters, first place the glass on a table holding it by the stem and rotate it in small circles. Once you get the hang of it, you can do it off the table while holding the glass in mid air. BE CAREFUL. I have seen many people attempt swirling and end up throwing the wine all over their own and the next person's shirt.

Wine tasting can be broken down simply into **Appearance**, **Smell** and **Taste.**

APPEARANCE

A wine's appearance can be the first indicator of what you are about to taste. Appearance can be further divided into 3 elements, which are: *Color Intensity, Color Hue, and Clarity*

Color Intensity

The color intensity of a wine will indicate if a wine is full, medium, or light bodied. For red wines, deeper color is *usually* better, but this is not necessarily true. Some Pinot Noir can be so light, they are almost see-through

Color Hue

Colors obviously vary for red and white wines. The various colors are:

White Wines:
Pale green to yellow : Typical of younger wines, especially those made from grapes grown in cooler climates.

Straw color : The typical color of white wines recently released to the market.

Yellow Gold: Typical color of older, white wine and young, sweet dessert wines.

Gold : Typical color for older, aged white wine and fuller bodied, dessert wines.

Brown: This color could mean that the white wine has gone bad.
Usually, only Sherry should have this color.

Red Wines:
Purple : The color of very young wine.

Ruby : Typical color of dry, red wines and young, Port wines.

Brick Red : Indicates that the wine is maturing.

Red to Brown : The stage at which dry red wines can start to turn bad, however, definitely still drinkable.

Tawny : The wine has gone bad. Only Tawny Port wines should have this color.

Amber Brown : Another indicator that the wine has gone bad. Only Sherry wines should have this color.

Clarity

Wine should generally not have any cloudiness or haziness, which mean the wine is flawed.

SMELL

What you smell is what you get. Smell and taste are closely connected. After analyzing the appearance, you must swirl the wine in your glass. This allows the aromas to open up and then you start to smell. Put your nose inside the glass, not all the way, and inhale gently. You may smell hints of fruits such as oranges, lemon, pineapple, grapefruit, apple, peach, apricot, banana, plus hundreds of others, for white wines. For red wines, you may smell blackberries, cherries, cassis, tar, chocolate, prunes, licorice, tobacco, plus a million more.

TASTE

Here we go, the last and most decisive step---tasting the wine. Smelling the wine can tell you a lot, but tasting will allow you to fully evaluate it. Take a small sip and swirl it around in your mouth. This swirling allows the tongue to take in all the wine's flavors. For bigger red wines, chewing the wine may be more appropriate than swirling it in your mouth. Sucking in a little air, while the wine is in your mouth, allows the aromas and tastes to come out more. Now, swallow the wine and take notice to how it tastes and with what impression it might leave you.

You should judge the wine by:
Sweetness/Dryness, Acidity, Body, Tannins, Alcohol, Bitterness, Finish, Balance

SWEETNESS/DRYNESS

Red wines are almost always vinified completely dry. Some white wines made from grapes such as Rieslings, Gewurztraminer, and Chenin Blanc have just a slight touch of sweetness, due to the residual sugar. Sweetness is detected at the tip of the tongue and must be balanced by high acidity. The more sugar a grape has, the more aroma and flavor. Pretty simple stuff, huh? Dessert wines are very sweet and have a good amount of residual sugar. Sometimes, over-oaked wines such as New World Chardonnays give off hints of sweetness. This sweetness appears as a vanilla-like flavor, imparted from the oak barrels.

ACIDITY

Very important component of wine. It is detected by its tartness and should be relatively high, especially for white wines. The acidity is a wine's backbone. The higher the acidity, the longer the ageing capability. If the acidity is high, you get a wine with life that is food friendly. The acidity also acts as a preservative. Wines with high acidity are Riesling, Chianti, and Sauvignon Blanc, just to name a few of the many. Of course, overly-aggressive acidity is annoying and a flaw.

BODY

A wine's body is judged by its texture and weight in the mouth. This texture and weight are a combination of extract, alcohol, and acid. If the wine feels rich and heavy in the mouth, then it is full bodied. A lighter, crispy, almost watery wine would be considered a light bodied wine. Medium bodied wines fall somewhere in the middle of the two. Dessert wines tend to be fuller bodied because the residual sugar adds weight and texture. That is why a grape such as Riesling is so amazing. Even if made into a dessert wine, Riesling has such high acidity that the wine feels light as a feather in the mouth. The acidity counters the grape's sugars.

TANNINS

Tannins are astringent substances most often found in red wines. The tannins usually come from the grapes' skins, seeds, and stems, as well as the oak barrels in which they may be aged. Tannins appear rough in the mouth but soften if the wine is given time to age. Tannins, as well as acidity, give wines good structure. Wines that are tannic are Cabernet Sauvignon, Sagrantino, and Barolo, just to name a few.

ALCOHOL

Excess alcohol is easily noticed and is unfortunately all too common in New World wines. Excess alcohol gives your mouth a hot feeling. Alcoholic wines are a terrible match with spicy foods.

BITTERNESS
The word bitterness is thrown around today like it's a Frisbee. Bordeaux wines are not bitter. They are earthy (a positive characteristic). True bitterness is a detriment and can be easily detected at the back of the mouth.

FINISH
The finish of a wine is the impression it leaves you with after it has been swallowed. If the wine's impression remains with you for quite a while, then it is called a long finish. If the wine's impression disappears after being swallowed, then the finish is short.

BALANCE
My favorite word. All of a wine's components must be judged by their relationships to each other. If none of the components overpower each other, then the wine is well balanced. Too many New World wines can be easily dissected. None of the flavors seem to integrate. It is almost as if there were a separation between each element. If a wine has a lot of fruit, then it must have a lot of acidity to back it up. There must be a yin yang relationship to present a wine with pure harmony.

N.B. : Tannins Vs. Acidity
No two things are so often misunderstood and swapped out for each other when it comes to analyzing and discussing wine than Tannins and Acidity. Tannins and Acidity are not the same thing. Tannins are astringent substances that dry out the mouth. Think Green tea with no sugar or honey. Try to envision how your mouth feels when drinking it. Acidity is what you find in a lemon; try to envision drinking lemon juice or, less severe, lemonade. When explaining this to customers / students, I even make faces to show how my mouth looks when I have green tea and how I pucker when I have something tangy and slightly sour (for lack of a better word) when I have lemonade.

GENERAL WINE TERMS

ACIDITY: Acidity is noted in a wine by a tart feeling in the mouth. High acidity is a good thing, regardless of what some people may say. It gives a wine life and it keeps things interesting. Excessive acidity is not great but it's better than flat tasting, oak juice. The acidity brings out the flavors in a wine and the food you are eating. There are many kinds of acids, the main ones being: malic acid, tartaric acid, and lactic acid. Malic acid gives tastes of raw green apples. Tartaric acid has a more ripe, citrus taste. Lactic acid is rounder and it dulls the wine. Lactic acid is like milk. Obviously, malic acid is the best, especially in white wines.

AERATION: To air out a wine, usually red wine. The aeration process opens up the wine and softens it. The aerating of wine can be exercised either by decanting or by swirling in a glass. European red wines, especially older ones, benefit highly from aeration.

AGEING: The process of ageing allows the wine to mature and develop flavors. It can round out the sharp edges. The tannins soften and occasionally shed to become sediment, along with dead yeast cells. Certain red wines must be aged. White wines, on the other hand, are not always meant to age. Of all white wines, Rieslings are the most age worthy, thanks to its high level of acidity. It would be better if almost all white wines were aged in stainless steel tanks and not oak barrels. Ageing in oak barrels softens the wine much more than stainless steel. Oak barrels give off tannins and the trademark hints of vanilla. The toasty flavors in wine also come from ageing in oak barrels. The smaller the oak barrel, the more of its flavor it imparts on the wine. Stainless steel lets the wine keep its freshness, making it not as soft as oak aged wine. The wine may be further aged in the bottle before its release.

ALCOHOLIC: A term that describes a high alcohol wine that tastes hot in the mouth.

ANTHOCYANINS: The pigments found in the grape that give wine its red color.

APPASSIMENTO: A process in which the grapes are semi-dried, losing almost half of their water content. As a result, the sugars become concentrated and, therefore, the flavors are intensified. Passito refers to wines made by this process. This is the very same process that produces the world famous and exceptionally unique Amarone wines.

APPELLATION: A designated wine growing area that is governed by certain laws specific to each country.
France has **AOC** (Appellation D'Origine Controlée)
Italy has both **DOC** (Denominazione Di Origine Controllata) *and*
DOCG (Denominazione Di Origine Controllata e Garantita)
Spain has **DO** (Denominacio de Origen)
Portugal has **DOC** (Denominacao De Origem Controlada)
The United States has **AVA** (American Viticultural Area)

AROMA: What you smell in the glass. The term "bouquet" is sometimes used to describe the aroma in older, aged wine.

AROMATIC: When a wine has dominant notes on the nose.

BARREL: A wooden container that is used to store and age the wine. Oak is the most popular used wood for barrels.

BARRIQUE: A 225-liter, oak barrel that is much smaller than older, more traditional oak barrels. The small size imparts more of the oak's flavors and components to the wine.

BIG: A term to describe a wine that is full bodied and rich. The flavors are concentrated and intense. New World wines tend to be bigger than big and, therefore, seem clumsy and without balance.

BITTER: Too many people confuse this term. A wine is bitter if it went bad. Some wines can have positive attributes such as bitter chocolate or bitter cherries. A wine novice would drink Bordeaux and deem it bitter. European wines tend to be earthy, not bitter.

BLENDING: To combine different wines to create a certain flavor profile. This profile would not be possible had only one grape been used. The blend may use juice from different grape varieties, different years, different regions, different countries, or from different barrels. An example is blending Merlot to add softness to a big tannic Cabernet Sauvignon wine.

BODY: The feel of the wine in the mouth. The weight and texture are judged to see if the wine is full, medium, or light bodied. Light bodied wines can be perceived as watery and well, light. Full bodied wines are rich and heavy in the mouth. Medium bodied wines are somewhere in between. Many dessert wines are considered full bodied because of the residual sugar, which adds weight and texture.

BOTRYTIS CINEREA: A fungus that grows on the grape and can be of great benefit. Under the perfect circumstances, the fungus can cause the grape to boost its own sugar levels. In this case, Botrytis Cinerea is called noble rot and the wines are made into beautiful dessert wines. Gray rot, on the other hand, is bad and ruins the grape.

BOUQUET: The aroma of a wine, typically an aged and mature wine.

BREATHE: The wine breathes as soon as it is exposed to air. Decanting a wine into a decanter allows it to fully open. The wine softens and opens up. The initial, funky taste and smell of some wines can actually wear off and expose good, bold fruit. This aeration process is essential for most European, red wines, especially older ones.

BRIGHT: A fresh fruitiness enhanced by a higher level of acidity.

BRUT: The driest category for Champagne.

BUTTERY: A term used to describe a buttery smell and taste in a wine, usually New World Chardonnay. Either oak ageing or malolactic fermentation may bring about this buttery hint, or both. Personally, buttery white wine makes me sick just typing it. White wine should be crisp, not buttery.

CASSIS: A term used to describe the taste and smell of black currants in a wine. Typical of Cabernet Sauvignon based wines.

CEDAR: A term used to describe a taste and smell of cedar wood in wine. Cigar Box is a synonym. Some red wines can possess this positive attribute. If a white wine has this hint, then it was aged in oak barrels and that's usually a no-no.

CHEWY: A term used to describe a dense and rich wine. These full-bodied wines are almost always red, or at least they *should be*. They are meaty enough to be considered chewy.

CLASSICO: The Italian word for classic. It is meant to describe an area within a wine region that usually has the oldest wine tradition and best wines.

CLEAN: Drink German Rieslings and you'll understand this term better.

CLOSED: A wine that does not expose its character. Time for ageing may be necessary for the wine to open up.

CORKED: A wine that went bad due to a faulty cork is referred to as corked. Up to 7% of all wines are, unfortunately, corked. If people eventually get over the useless tradition of cork, wineries will switch to screw caps and we can all enjoy good wine that never spoils.

CRAP: This is not an *official* wine term, but when you taste crappy wine, what else are you supposed to say? Synonymous with: Junk, S#*t, Is this a joke?, Gasoline, etc.

CRISP: A description for highly acidic wine. The acidity does wonders for wine, especially white wine.

DEEP: The intensity and depth of a wine.

DELICATE: Wines of great quality that are delicate, elegant, and refined.

DEMI-SEC: French word for "half dry".

DOUX: French word for "sweet".

DRY: A term to describe a wine that has had all its sugars converted to alcohol. Most beginners fear the word sweet and think dry is good. That is half true and half false. Most wines are dry. A wine novice who asks for a dry wine actually desires a sweet wine. They crave California Chardonnay, which are so oaked that they are sweet. The oak imparts a sweet vanilla flavor to the wine. These wines are made dry but taste sweet and so considering a California Chardonnay to be dry is *somewhat* contradictory.

EARTHY: A term to describe a wine that displays hints of earth and damp soil. This is considered a positive attribute in red wines.

ELEGANT: A term for wines that are delicate and exude finesse.

EUCALYPTUS: A term used to describe a mint-like aroma and taste in a red wine.

FERMENTATION: The natural process in which the yeasts (primarily found in the grape skins) convert the grape juice into wine. The yeasts help convert the grapes' sugars into alcohol and carbon dioxide. The carbon dioxide usually escapes via the air. In making Champagne, the carbon dioxide is trapped purposefully to create its characteristic effervescence.

FILTERING: A process in which the wine is filtered to improve clarification just before bottling. The filtering process removes yeast cells and other unwanted particles. It also removes sediment. Some winemakers believe that filtering may remove some flavor that the sediment offers to the wine. These producers label their wines "Unfiltered". It is typical to find deposits of sediments on the bottom of "Unfiltered" bottles or in your glass. Do not panic; it is harmless and it will not kill you. Fining is a similar process.

FINESSE: The trademark of German Rieslings. Finesse is a term used to describe a wine that is elegant, graceful, and well balanced.

FINISH: A wine's finish is the impression it leaves in your mouth after it is swallowed. The taste and texture may linger and this is referred to as a long finish.

FIRM: This is self-explanatory. It describes a wine that has a good amount of tannins and a high level of acidity, but still well balanced.

FLABBY: Another self-explanatory term. The opposite of firm. Flabby wines lack the main source of life: acidity. These wines are usually oaked to add some interest, but I am not fooled easily.

FLAT: A synonym for Flabby.

FLESHY: A term used to describe a full-bodied wine that is high in extract and alcohol. A synonym for Chewy and the opposite of Lean.

FLINT: A positive characteristic of very dry white wines. It is a term that describes the smell and taste of flint striking steel. Typical of French wines such as Chablis and Sancerre.

FLORAL: Floral wines have aromas of flowers. Pretty simple, huh?

FORTIFIED WINE: A wine that has had extra alcohol or brandy (in most cases) added to boost the alcohol level up to at least 17%. Port, Madeira, Marsala, and Sherry are fortified wines.

FRESH: A wine that is alive, thanks to the acidity. It is used for clean and bright wines.

FRIZZANTE: The Italian word for "lightly sparkling". The next step in effervescence is Spumante.

FRUITY: Describes wine that are, well, fruity. The wine can exhibit hints of any fruit. You name it. Even cooked fruit. Fruitiness must be backed by acidity to be presented in a well-balanced package.

GAMEY: A term to describe older red wines that display notes of game animals. It can seem borderline decayed and, for some, is an acquired taste.

GRAPEY: A term used for wines with reminiscent hints of raw grapes.

GRASSY: A term that describes the smell and taste of freshly cut grass. This is the most typical characteristic of Sauvignon Blanc wines.

GREEN: A term that holds many meanings. In one sense it might describe the grassy hints noted in white wine. It may also imply that a wine is not yet ready to drink and has a highly acidic, under-ripe taste.

GRIP: A term that typically describes red wine that has a firm grip. This is a result of a high level of acidity and tannins.

HERBACEOUS: A term to describe wines with a smell and taste of herbs (fresh or dried). A typical description for white Sauvignon Blanc and Cabernet Franc wines. Herbal is a synonymous term.

HONEYED: A term used to describe the honey-like fragrance and taste in a wine. Very typical of sweet Muscat wines and many other dessert wines.

INKY: The term which describes the "inky" deepness of some red wines.

JAMMY: A term to describe the concentrated, fruity aroma and taste of a wine.

LEATHERY: A term to describe the leather smell occasionally found in some big tannic reds. The leather hints are usually extracted from the oak barrels during ageing.

LIVELY: A term that is used to describe a wine that is fresh. The high level of acidity is what terms a wine lively.

LUSH: A descriptor for wines that are rich but still soft and velvety.

MACERATION: The amount of time that the grape juice stays in contact with the grape skins, seeds, and, sometimes, stems. The goal is to extract components, which would enhance the wine's texture, flavor, aroma, and color. Maceration for red wines is usually longer than the ones for white wines, while orange wines and rosé wines fall in the middle. Stems, seeds, and skins can sometimes contribute unwanted elements to white wine.

MALOLACTIC FERMENTATION: Also called Secondary Fermentation. This process converts malic acid into lactic acid. Malic acid is the one that is responsible for a wine's juiciness and is the life of the party. Lactic acid is soft, round, and dull. Acceptable for red wines, but should be a no-no for all white wines. Almost every New World Chardonnay, specifically Californian, undergoes malolactic fermentation. The little acidity in these wines is further dulled (eliminated, if you will) and then sentenced to the oak chamber of death. Lactic acid makes white wines taste like milk. Go ahead! Have a cup of that with your meal and throw up!

MATURE: A term that describes a wine that has fully developed from ageing and is ready to drink.

MEATY: A synonym for Chewy.

MINTY: A synonym for Eucalyptus.

NOBLE: A term that describes a wine with noble character. Drink good Vino Nobile di Montepulciano and you will understand this term better.

NOBLE ROT: A synonym for the good strain of Botrytis Cinerea.

NOSE: A term that describes the wine's aroma or bouquet.

NUTTY: A descriptor for wines with a nutty characteristic. Good sign for Sherry, but a too common problem for California Chardonnays due to excessive oak flavoring.

OAK: Oak is the wood of choice for barrels used in ageing wine. The oak imparts flavors and even gives tannins. This is a good thing for red wines. For white wines, it spoils everything and turns the wine sweet, with vanilla and toast tastes. It can be essential for certain reds, but can mask certain flaws in a white wine. Unfortunately, for some winemakers, the oak itself can be a flaw. Wines like these are termed "oaked", which can be a positive or negative attribute, depending on the wine and your opinion.

OFF: A term that describes wine that has gone bad.

OFF DRY: A term for wine that has the slightest hint of sweetness.

OPEN: A wine that shows its offerings and is ready to drink. An open wine is the opposite of a closed wine. Older wines need time to open up. This is achieved by decanting.

OVERRIPE: A term for wine made from grapes that were left hanging way too long on the vine. The acidity is lost and the fruitiness is overbearing. It has sadly become a trend for New World wineries to make wine from overripe fruit. My advice: Save your money and buy a can of grape soda. It's the same thing but cheaper.

OXIDIZED: A term for wines that have been exposed to air for a long time. The air deteriorates the wine and renders it undrinkable. Oxidization is only a beneficial process for Sherry, Madeira, or Rivesaltes wines. In these cases, the air gives the wines their characteristic nutty-caramel flavor. There are rare exceptions for a few wines that benefit from oxidization.

POMACE: Pomace is what is left after the juice has been pressed from the grapes. The remaining elements are skins, seeds, and pulp. Sometimes the pomace is used to make Grappa or Eau de Vie.

POWERFUL: A term used to describe red wines that are full bodied, full flavored, and have a high level of alcohol.

RAISINY: A term used to describe rich and intensely concentrated wines. The term is usually applied to dessert wines. Amarone is one of the very few, dry, table wines that are usually referred to as raisiny.

RESIDUAL SUGAR: The remaining sugar that is either purposefully or involuntarily left in a wine after fermentation.

RICH: A term that describes wines which are full flavored, full bodied, and high in alcohol. Robust is a synonym.

RIPE: A term for wines made from grapes that have fully developed its flavors. The ripeness of a grape is achieved by leaving the grapes on the vine for a little while longer. There is one problem. As the grape ripens, it boosts its sugar levels, while the acidity level declines. A good winemaker should know when to pick the grapes so that both the sugars and acidity are in perfect balance. Very few grapes can pull this off. Riesling is such an incredible grape that it boasts high sugar levels as well as high acidity levels. It is like a genetic freak of nature given to us as a gift from up above.

ROSATO : The Italian word for Rosé.

ROSÉ: The French word for pink or rose colored. It refers to the wines of this color. White wines can be made from red grapes. When you squeeze a grape, the juice that comes out is clear, not colored. It is only when that pressed juice stays in contact with the grape skins, seeds, and pulps, in a process called maceration, that the wines gain color. Rosé wines are made from red grapes but the pressed juice is left in contact with the skins for only a short period of time. The result is a pink wine with a little more body, fruit, interest, and, of course, color. Rosé Champagne, on the other hand, is made by blending white and red wines. Rosé wines should be served chilled.

ROUGH: A term for wines too tough to drink. The roughness can soften if the wine is allowed time to age.

ROUND: A term for well balanced, full-bodied wines with no sharp edges.

SECOND LABEL: Second label wines are like a winery's runner up. The winery's second place nominee. The wines can usually be quite good and come at a lesser price.

SEDIMENT: The deposit at the bottom of the bottle or wine glass. Typically found in older red wines. When a wine ages, it loses some of its tannins and softens up. Those shed tannins, along with dead yeast cells, form the deposit known as sediment. Do not be alarmed. Sediment is harmless. It is very typically found in Port wine. Sediment can and should be easily removed. When decanting a wine, be careful to do it slowly, so that the sediment does not pour over from the bottle into the decanter.

SMOKY: When a wine displays smoky aromas or tastes. This smokiness may be inherent in the soil, which bears the vines, or may come from excessive ageing of the wine in oak barrels.

SPICY: A term for wines with aromas or tastes of spices like cloves, cinnamon, nutmeg, or pepper. The red grape Shiraz and the white grape Gewurztraminer are typically described as spicy.

SPUMANTE: The Italian word for sparkling. Spumante wines have more bubbles than Frizzante wines.

STEELY: Positive term to describee a white wine's lean body and high acidity.

STRUCTURE: Another self-explanatory term. It includes a wine's acidity, alcohol, fruit, body, tannins, etc. All wines have structure, it is just a question of it being well structured or not.

SWEET: Sweetness is detected on the tip of the tongue and comes from residual sugar left after fermentation. Sugar must be balanced by acidity, something not common in New World wines. Some grapes are intrinsically sweet and this sweetness is further exhibited in the wine. Sweetness can also come from ageing in oak barrels.

SYRUPY: A term that can be used to describe thick, sweet wines.

TANNINS: Tannins are astringent substances found in the grape skins, seeds, stems, and even the oak barrels in which they are aged. They give red wine flavor, texture, and structure. Tannins can also behave like antioxidants and allow the wines to age gracefully. With age, the tannins turn from rough to soft and are occasionally shed. These shed tannins, along with dead yeast cells, form a deposit at the bottom of the bottle called sediment. Wines with noticeable tannins are referred to as tannic. Tannins feel dry and puckery in the mouth and the back of the throat.

TAR: A descriptor for wines that smell of tar. Barolos typically display hints of tar.

TART: A wine that is high in acid. Crisp is a synonym.

TERROIR: The famous French term which literally means soil. Terroir is used to describe wine and is not only limited to soil. Terroir embodies everything. That is, every and anything that might influence the taste of the wine. Terroir includes the grapes, the soil, the amount of sun, the angle of the vineyard to the sun, the water drainage, the altitude, etc.

TEXTURE: Yet another self-explanatory term.

THICK: A self-explanatory term. Thick wines are dense and rich.

TOASTY: A term for wine with aromas and tastes of toasted bread. Toast hints come from ageing in oak barrels and are all too common for Californian Chardonnay.

TOBACCO: A term to describe the aroma of tobacco in some red wines such as Spanish Rioja.

UNFILTERED: Wine that has not been filtered. Unfiltered wines typically have sediment at the bottom of the bottle.

UNDERRIPE: A term for wine made with grapes that were picked not yet ripe. Such wines have high acidity and very little sugar levels.

VANILLA: A term for wines with vanilla-like aromas. This aroma is derived from ageing in oak barrels. Very common in New World wines. Sometimes, it is all you taste.

VARIETAL: A wine that uses the name of the main grape from which it is made. Very common practice for New World wines.

VEGETAL: A term that describes wines with aromas and tastes of vegetables such as bell peppers. This is typical of wines such as Cabernet Franc. Even Cabernet Sauvignon can be vegetal if the grapes are grown in cooler areas.

VINTAGE: A term that describes the year of the grape harvest and the wine made from those grapes. The word vintage wine is not intended to denote quality. Only in Port and Champagne does the word vintage specify quality.

WATERY: A very light bodied wine.

SERVING AND STORING WINE

Red wines are best served between 56 – 60 degrees Fahrenheit.

White wines are best served between 45 – 50 Fahrenheit.

Orange wines are best served between 45 – 50 Fahrenheit.

Rosé wines are best served between 45 – 50 Fahrenheit.

Good Champagne should never be served too cold. Optimum serving temperatures for good Champagne is between 48 – 52 Fahrenheit. Champagnes of lesser quality should be served colder.

Sweet Dessert wines are best served between 45 – 50 degrees Fahrenheit.

Fortified wines are best served between 55 – 60 degrees Fahrenheit.

Cognacs, Armagnacs, and other Brandies are best served between 55- 60 degrees Fahrenheit.

Grappa is best served between 45 –50 degrees Fahrenheit.

Wine should be stored in a cool dark place. Wine hates heat, light, and vibration.

Storing **LEFTOVER** wine is always confusing to most people. The best thing to do is pour the remaining wine in smaller wine bottles, known as half bottles or splits. This will minimize the amount of air in contact with the wine. The next thing to do is get something called a vacuum wine saver. This gadget takes out roughly 60% of the remaining air. If the wine is white, put it back in the fridge. For red wine, store it in a cool place. Another option is a spray, made of inert gas, that removes the oxygen.

THE WINE COUNTRIES

*Buenos Aires

1) Salta
2) La Rioja
3) Mendoza
4) Patagonia

ARGENTINA

ARGENTINA

Argentina is one of the few places in South America that produces wine. Argentina has many residents of European lineages, particularly Spanish and Italian. These European immigrants have brought with them their love and need for wine. Argentina *used* to produce a lot of wine but nothing of quality. New producers came in and drastically changed that. The country does well with international varieties. This is a good thing because they have no choice but to import foreign grapes. Argentina barely has any indigenous grapes of any significant importance. Argentine wines are great values.

**The main regions to know are :
Mendoza, Salta, La Rioja,
and Patagonia.**

Mendoza

The overwhelming majority of all grapes grown in Argentina are grown in Mendoza, where winemakers mostly plant **Malbec and Cabernet Sauvignon**. The two French grapes are more fruit-driven than they are when made in their birthplace. The Malbec in particular is made more accessible. Malbec wines are known as "black" and some used to deem it undrinkable, but Mendoza Malbecs proved the doubters wrong. Since the first writing of this book in 2002 to now, almost 20 years later, Malbec is one of America's most popular red wines. The perfect match for Malbec is beef, Argentina's number one food. Enjoy it with their famous mixed grill, a parrillada.

Salta and La Rioja

Salta and La Rioja are both in Northern Argentina and gaining much attention. Salta is one of the World's highest altitude regions for winemaking and its **Cafayate sub-region** makes some of the best wines in the country. Salta makes fantastic Malbec and also white wine from the grape **Torrontés**. La Rioja does very well with Torrontés, too. It's a grape that tastes as if it were a cross between Sauvignon Blanc and Viognier, with flavors of peach, apricot, pear, melon, and honey.

Patagonia

Patagonia is the southern portion of Argentina and **Rio Negro**, a province, makes the best wines of the area.

★ Canberra
1) Margaret River
2) Barossa Valley
3) Coonawarra
4) Yarra Valley
5) Hunter Valley

AUSTRALIA

AUSTRALIA

Australia has had vineyards for a very long time, but quality wine is a relatively new phenomenon, starting in the 1990's. Australia has no indigenous grapes of any importance. They rely on trustworthy and, obviously very marketable, international varieties. One variety in particular, Shiraz, does very well. Shiraz is the Australian term for the French grape Syrah. Australia also plants large amounts of Cabernet Sauvignon, Merlot, and Chardonnay. There are also other varieties planted but none do as well as the above mentioned.

Australia is huge but most of its vineyards, and the best ones, are located in the South East. Australian wines are considered New World; the style is big, oaky, fruity, and alcoholic. Too many Australian wines, like many in the New World, are ridiculously monstrous and do not match well with too many foods. As with other New World wines, if you had one wine…you probably had them all. That being said, Australia makes some terrific wines that are world class are worthy of your attention. Lookout for artisanal, wine producers who make wines which speak of the land and people. **The main wine areas are** :

SOUTHWEST
Margaret River

SOUTHEAST
Hunter Valley
Yarra Valley
Coonawarra
Barossa Valley

SOUTHWEST

MARGARET RIVER
Relatively new wine zone producing **Cabernet Sauvignon, Merlot, Shiraz, and Chardonnay** etc. Not much to talk about. Try some and then move on with your life.

SOUTHEAST

HUNTER VALLEY
This is where you get GOOD Australian wine. World famous for the **Shiraz** produced in this area. **Semillon and Chardonnay** are very popular white grapes here. The Shiraz from Hunter Valley is best served with red meat.

YARRA VALLEY
Best known for its red wines like **Pinot Noir and Cabernet Sauvignon**. The Pinot Noir goes best with poultry and other light white meats while the Cabernet stands up well to red meat.

COONAWARRA
Famous area that produces primarily **Cabernet Sauvignon and Shiraz** for reds and **Chardonnay** for white.

BAROSSA VALLEY
The Barossa Valley makes a lot of **Riesling** wine, none of which compares to the incredible German stuff. The reds are **Grenache and Shiraz** blends that most resemble fruit driven versions of a French Côtes du Rhône.

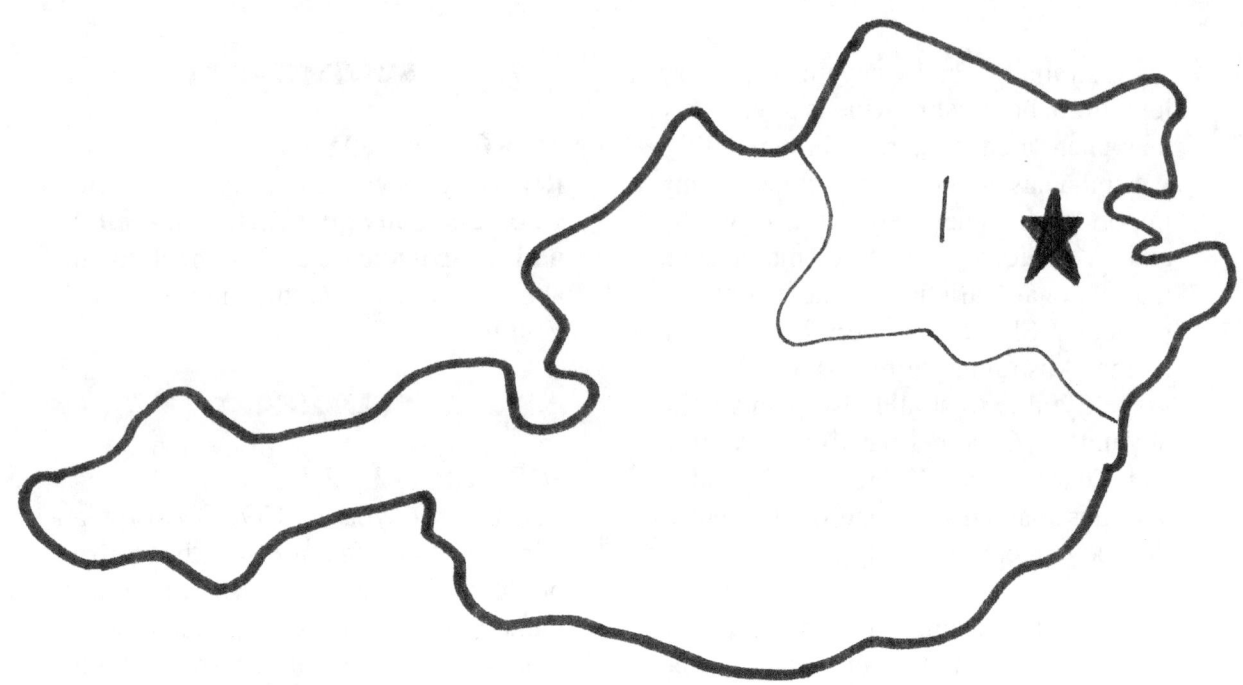

★ Vienna
1) Niederosterreich

AUSTRIA

AUSTRIA

Austria is one of the last places a wine novice thinks about when buying wine, or even discussing it for that matter. Why? I ask. The same goes for Germany. Enter the mind of a wine fanatic and you will discover Austria usually occupies a seat on his/her Top 5 list, especially and specifically for white wine. The wines of Austria can be very similar to those of Germany. They both plant similar grapes like Riesling and Gewurztraminer. The weather in Austria is cool but a little hotter than Germany. This Austrian climate produces Rieslings and Gewurztraminers that are bigger, drier, more full-bodied, and with a higher level of alcohol than those of Germany.

The native grape Gruner Veltliner is a wine lover's gift from God. This gift, however, usually does not come cheap. It is unfortunate that Austrian wine is very hard to find outside of Austria. To make it worse, people don't give Austrian wine a chance. To make it even worse, retailers and restaurants usually do not know anything about Austrian wines. Go ahead. Go into a wine store and ask for Austrian wines. They will look at you confused. Most don't even know Austria made wine. Most don't even know where Austria is located! Most will confuse Austria with Australia and point you to a shelf full of overoaked Shiraz. My point is, even if you were interested in Austrian wine, which you should be, you probably won't find much. I have decided to make my chapter on Austrian wine short and brief, because what's the point anyway? The good news is, those of us in the know have Austrian wines all for ourselves.

Most of the Austrian wines are white, with a notable red exception, and are made in the eastern part in a region called **Niederosterreich**.

RIESLING
The Rieslings of Austria are bigger, drier, and have a higher level of alcohol than the German ones. Hints of peaches are also present and, as always, these Rieslings are incredibly food friendly. Great with pork and cabbage dishes.

GEWURZTRAMINER
Another typical grape from Germany makes its way over here and does well. As is the case with Austrian Rieslings, the Gewurztraminers here are bigger, drier, and also have a higher level of alcohol. Great with spicy foods.

GRUNER VELTLINER
Gruner Veltliner is Austria's pride and joy. The grape is kind of like Riesling but totally different, if you know what I mean. It tastes as if it were a cross between Pinot Grigio and Sauvignon Blanc. Gruner typically displays hints of peach, white pepper, and even is herbaceous, with hints of celery. This wine is high in acidity and leaves your mouth feeling clean and refreshed. Perfect with fish and shellfish. Great with green vegetables as well as poultry and other white meats.

ZWEIGELT
Zweigelt is most likely Austria's most planted red grape. It's like a Pinot Noir but heftier, with peppery flavors of dark cherry.

★ Sacramento
1) Mendocino
2) Sonoma
3) Napa
4) Monterey
5) Paso Robles
6) Edna Valley
7) Santa Rita
8) Santa Ynez

CALIFORNIA

CALIFORNIA

California has entered the wine market and took it by storm. As impressive as this whirlwind of new style wines may be, do not forget that storms will always leave damage behind. California wine can be really great, just as it can be utterly disgusting. It seems to be the land of wine extremes. Quality, unfortunately, does not come cheap, thanks to a very expensive climate in which to do business. Audacious prices are sometimes charged for quite ordinary stuff. That being said, when the wines are good, they're worth coughing up the money. It's a great feeling when you give back to a State that gave this country and World so much.

There are some amazing wines I have tried from California but these typically come at high prices. If you really want to challenge yourself, find an amazing $15 bottle (in 2019 prices) of California red or white that tastes *unique*. I am willing to bet you would return empty handed. California wineries are waking up and are promising to implement changes. They realize the potential California has to produce great wine and are attempting to devise a way to offer these wines at lower prices. For a few bucks more, you can find wines that speak of their terroir and the hard work of the winemakers.

Most of the wines are made from famous international varieties such as: Cabernet Sauvignon, Merlot, Pinot Noir, Shiraz, Chardonnay, Sauvignon Blanc, etc. Zinfandel is a widely planted grape that was once thought to be native to California, but has later been discovered to be a descendant of Italy's Primitivo grape. I would say it's my favorite, unique American wine and the only one I don't mind if it's too fruity.

Stay away from the California wines that are too big, too fruity, too alcoholic, and too much of everything else. These wines are meant for immediate gratification. California can soar to the top if they just take advantage of what they have at their disposal : great land, climate, and extremely caring and hard working wine people. I love everything about California and would love to see the state maximize its wine potential. The land and people are great; there just needs to be a shift in the focus and I believe it will benefit producers across the board, especially smaller ones. More importantly, the consumer will win.

California boasts many wine regions. **The main ones** to know are broken down geographically as :

NORTH COAST
Mendocino County
Sonoma Valley
Napa Valley

CENTRAL COAST
Monterey County
Paso Robles
Edna Valley
Santa Rita
Santa Ynez

NORTH COAST

MENDOCINO COUNTY

Mendocino County has many wine areas but the one to know is **Anderson Valley**. Anderson Valley is cooler than most California's wine areas and does well with **Chardonnay**. The acidity is higher and the grapes do not become over ripe like most others in the state. Many reds are also made but the focus seems to be on the white Chardonnay grape.

SONOMA VALLEY

Sonoma has quite a few wine areas but the main ones to know are:

Alexander Valley, Dry Creek Valley
Russian River Valley, Sonoma Valley
Carneros

ALEXANDER VALLEY

This area can produce great **Cabernet and Chardonnay** grapes. Many producers from around California buy their grapes from Alexander Valley. The region can be quite hot so Cabernets and Chardonnays are picked pretty ripe. The region also does well with many other grapes such as **Zinfandel and Merlot**.

DRY CREEK VALLEY

Dry Creek is hotter in the North, so it can produce good **Zinfandel**, while the South's cool weather produces good **Chardonnay** grapes.

RUSSIAN RIVER VALLEY

This wine region is quite cool and can produce some great **Chardonnay**. French owned companies also produce some sparkling wine here.

SONOMA VALLEY

Does very well with **Cabernet and Zinfandel**. Mostly warm weather except in the South.

CARNEROS VALLEY

The southern portion of the Sonoma Valley is quite cool and can produce some good **Chardonnay**.

NAPA VALLEY

THE most famous wine region in the United States. The northern part has cooler weather than the southern portion. Wherever you go in this region, you will realize that Napa *is* **Cabernet Sauvignon**. It is wildly popular here and can produce the best in the whole state. The best of Napa can rival even the best in the world. Some of the most expensive wines of America come out of Napa Valley.

CENTRAL COAST

MONTEREY COUNTY
Chardonnay reigns supreme in this cool weathered wine region. Riesling is also very popular, although the best examples are equal to average German Rieslings.

PASO ROBLES
A hot region that primarily produces **Cabernet** and, of course, **Zinfandel**. The wines tend to be very alcoholic

EDNA VALLEY
The cool weather is ideal for great **Chardonna**y, if it is not excessively bathed in oak barrels. Also makes some of California's better **Pinot Noir**.

SANTA RITA
One of California's best regions for outstanding Pinot Noir.

SANTA YNEZ
Quite possibly California's most beautiful area makes, quite possibly, the state's best Pinot Noir. They are also known for Rhône blends.

CHILE

This country burst onto the wine scene about two decades ago. They were greeted with tremendous enthusiasm and appreciated for their outstanding value. Low prices kept Chile, and many consumers, smiling, but, after a while, people started sobering up. They asked themselves, "How much **Cabernet and Merlot** can I drink?" They also started to realize that, although buying good Chilean wine could be a fun and inexpensive experience, it could be quite repetitive and boring. That being said, Chilean wines are great and inexpensive additions to any wine cellar. It's a good thing there are these affordable but still great wines on the global market.

The main standout they have is the red grape, **Carménère**, found mostly in the Colchagua region. Carménère, is not my favorite grape but some people seem to love it for its bell pepper and tobacco hints. This herbaceous-flavored red grape is originally from France but does well in Chile. Many foreign investors from France, the U.S., and even Spain rushed to Chile to plant vineyards by the mile. Chilean wine can be good and satisfying, but remember they are New World wines and the aim is immediate gratification. The wines are usually huge and fruity.

Chile has **two main wine areas**:

Maipo Valley
Colchagua

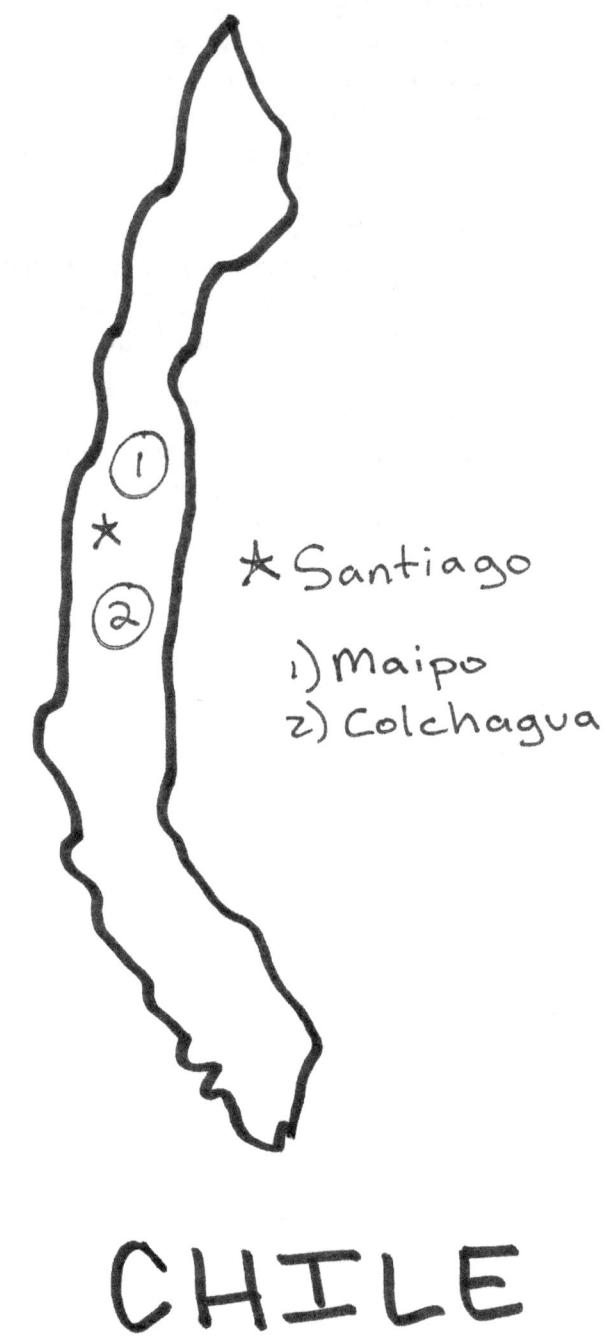

CROATIA

Though many wineries around the World get their oak to make wine barrels from Slavonia, in northeastern Croatia, no one, sadly, ever thinks of the wine in Croatia! The country is physically beautiful and has a proud people and great wine making potential.

Croatia has **2 main wine producing regions**, with many sub-regions.
The 2 main ones are :
Primorska (Coastal)
and
Kontinentalna (Continental).

Primorska
The coastal area (Primorska) produces wines that can be similar to nearby Friuli, Italy, but have quite a bit of catching up to do to reach that level. In fact, a few Friulian grapes make their way to Croatia under different names. Ribolla Gialla (**Jarbola** in Croatian), Refosco (**Refosk** in Croatian), and Terrano, which may or may not be Croatia's **Terran**, all are found here. With dedication and time, I believe their wines, especially whites, can become appreciated for their quality.

The best sub-areas of Primorska on the coast are **Istria and Dalmatia**. The Dalmatian coast is known for **Plavac Mali**, which is very closely related to Italy's Primitivo and California's Zinfandel. Dalmatia makes whites from **Posip**, which are crisp and citrusy. Istria makes **Malvazija**, a Malvasia subvariety, which is aromatic.

Kontinentaalna
The best of Kontinentalna is in **Slavoni**a. It's a region known for their white wines, especially from **Grasevina** (A.K.A. Welschriesling), the country's most planted white grape, that makes aromatic wines.

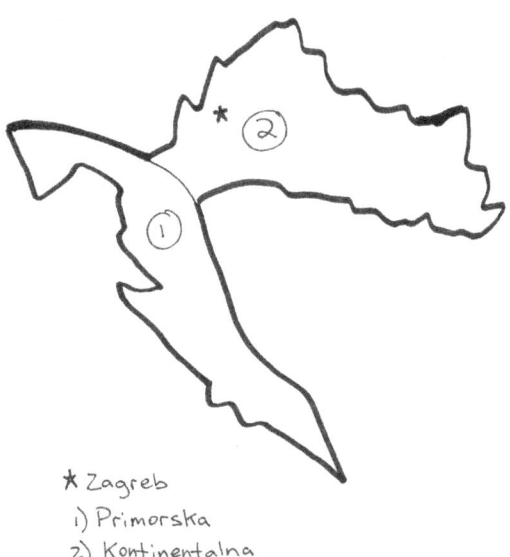

* Zagreb
1) Primorska
2) Kontinentalna

CROATIA

CZECH REPUBLIC

I'm so old school, I still call this country Czechoslovakia. My neighborhood, where I grew up in and where my wine store is located, used to be heavily Czech. The Czech Consulate is even a block away from us. We still proudly sell Czech liquors that are impossible to find and love it when people of Czech descent come from all over to buy them from In Vino Veritas. The Czech Republic is known for making the world's best beers; Germany would be second. As great as their beers are, attention should be paid to their wines. They are clean, like the beers they produce, and satisfying, like the fare enjoyed with them.

There are **2 main wine regions** : **Bohemia** (north west) and **Moravia** (south east).
Moravia is the best region and produces the most wine.

Moravia does well with **Riesling, Pinot Blanc, Gruner Veltliner, and Welschriesling**. It also makes a great **Rivaner** (A.K.A. Muller Thurgau), which is a very aromatic and crisp wonderful white.

Reds are often made from **Saint Laurent**, which may be related to Pinot Noir and Zweigelt and tastes like both.

★ Prague
1) Bohemia
2) Moravia

CZECH REPUBLIC

★ Paris
1) Champagne
2) Alsace
3) Burgundy
4) Loire
5) Cognac
6) Bordeaux
7) Madiran
8) Armagnac
9) Cahors
10) Rhône
11) Languedoc Roussillon
12) Provence
13) Corsica

FRANCE

FRANCE

France has long been the standard bearer in the wine world. Almost all of the famed, international varieties hail originally from France. Here, however, the grapes do not taste as they do in the New World. The grapes offer earthier hints and are less fruity. French wines are meant to go with French food. With a lengthy history and proud traditions under its belt, France has played the role model through out much of wine's history. France has perfected the art of living or *joie de vivre*. The French winegrowers should be considered breeders. They simply took wine to the next level.

The French are credited with inventing numerous terms, terroir being one of the very important. The literal meaning of terroir is soil, but it is meant to imply much more. Terroir implies everything, such as the water, the grapes, the slopes, the weather, the angle to the sun, the cultivation, the soil, etc, etc.

The Romans brought their viticulture to France. Since then, the love affair the French have with wine has developed into one of the country's many cultural foundations. This love affair went forward and produced, throughout history, the most elaborate classification of wines, specifically in the region called Bordeaux. The French have, over time, figured out which grapes grow perfectly in the right place. They have stuck with these guidelines and have obviously reaped the rewards and gained maximum success.

This success has unfortunately inflated certain people's egos and led the greedy to charge astronomical prices for wine even during bad years. Some of the most prestigious wineries have, in bad years, turned out wine that is not worth a third of their already ridiculously high asking price. With all that said, I urge people to learn about French wines and their well-organized system of wine classification. Many, almost all to be exact, French wines should be consumed with food.

NORTHWEST:
LOIRE

NORTHEAST:
CHAMPAGNE, ALSACE

CENTRAL WEST:
BORDEAUX, COGNAC

CENTRAL EAST:
BURGUNDY

SOUTHWEST:
CAHORS, MADIRAN, ARMAGNAC

SOUTHEAST:
RHÔNE, PROVENCE, LANGUEDOC-ROUSSILLON

ISLAND:
CORSICA

Many French wine regions are further divided into districts or subdivisions. The wines may be named after the town, district, or, very rarely, by grape. The regions listed above, all have subdivisions and districts. Listed below will **only be the major ones**. Including all of them would be long and quite boring.

NORTHWEST

LOIRE

Whites : Pouilly Fumé, Sancerre, Vouvray, Muscadet,
Rosé : Anjou
Red : Chinon

Whites

Pouilly Fumé
Fumé means smoke and describes the character of the wine made by **Sauvignon Blanc**. Sauvignon Blanc here is crisp and acidic, with grassy and herbaceous tones. Pouilly Fumé is getting pricier by the year. Do not confuse this with Pouilly Fuissé, a totally different wine made from the white grape Chardonnay.

Sancerre
Sancerre is famous for its white wine made from **Sauvignon Blanc**. Strikingly similar to the whites of nearby Pouilly Fumé, Sancerre is actually considered to be THE place for Sauvignon Blanc. Red wine made from **Pinot Noir** is also produced, but not as good as the Sancerre whites. The most important part of wine enjoyment is matching it with the food of the very same region where it is made. The Loire Valley is famous for its goat cheeses; Sauvignon Blanc wines and goat cheese are the absolute perfect marriage of food and wine. Try it and I guarantee you will agree.

Vouvray
From the grape called **Chenin Blanc**. Unique tastes of green apples with high acidity, and a welcomed, slight sweetness. Very minerally, it's great with shellfish, fried seafood, pork, or chicken. Can be made into sweet dessert wines and even into sparkling wine.

Muscadet
This white grape is also known as **Melon de Bourgogne**. These wines can be fairly average. The best are **Muscadet de Sevre-et-Maine**. Even better, look for these wines with the words *mise en bouteille sur lie* written on the label. That phrase indicates the wine was kept on the lees, meaning it was kept in contact with the dead yeast cells and not filtered, in order to enrich the flavor. These wines have nice hints of lemon and orange. They are generally softer with a slightly creamier mouth-feel. Great with shellfish.

Rosé

Anjou
Famous for two rosé wines: **Rosé D'Anjou and Cabernet D'Anjou**. Rosé D'Anjou is made primarily from Malbec and Gamay. Cabernet D'Anjou is made from Cabernet Franc and Cabernet Sauvignon.

Reds

Chinon
THE red of the Loire Valley. Made primarily from the **Cabernet Franc** grape. Chinon wines are typically lighter but some examples are able to age for up to 10 years. Chinon has high acidity, with raspberry and black currant hints. Best known for its herbal, bell pepper taste.

NORTHEAST

CHAMPAGNE

Only sparkling wine from this region may legally be called Champagne. Located about one and a half hours (90 miles) northeast of Paris. The weather of Champagne is cool and unsuitable for many grapes, except ones like **Chardonnay, Pinot Meunier, and Pinot Noir**, among a few others. The cool weather prevents the grapes from fully ripening and developing a high level of sugar.

The acidity, however, is kept at a high level. The low sugar / high acidity balance is exactly what is needed for good Champagne. Champagne has approximately 50 million bubbles per glass; the more bubbles create a textured and creamy feel in the mouth. The bubbles are THE most important part of Champagne. The high acidity should allow your mouth to feel clean and refreshed after a sip of Champagne. Good Champagne should *never* be served too cold.

Vintage Champagne implies that the wine is made from the best grapes of a harvest from a specific year.

Non-Vintage Champagne is a blend of wines from at least 2 separate years.
Non Vintage Champagne is made the same every year. The type of Champagne you get will be almost exactly the same from year to year. Three of every four bottles of Champagne produced are Non Vintage.

Rosé Champagnes are made by adding a small amount of red wine to the blend or by leaving the red grape skins in the must during pressing to give off color, body, and fruit. Rosé Champagnes are generally better, although it is a matter of taste. These wines also cost more.

On the Champagne label, you will see either:

Brut, Extra Dry, Demi-Sec, or Doux. These terms describe the level of sweetness (Brut being bone dry, while Doux is sweet).

Champagne is one of the best choices for appetizers, fish, shellfish, and fried foods. Its high level of acidity gives Champagne the privilege of being very food friendly. NEVER serve Champagne in those flat saucer-like glasses. The flatness quickly eliminates the bubbles (the sole purpose of Champagne). You must always use tall, flute-shaped glasses. Also, never serve Champagne in either a chilled or wet glass; both lessen the top's desired "foam".

NORTHEAST (continued)

ALSACE

Whites
Riesling, Gewurztraminer
Pinot Gris, Pinot Blanc

Sparkling
Cremant D'Alsace

Whites

Riesling
The best white grape in the World finds a comfortable home here in Alsace (the French, Eastern region that borders Germany). These French Rieslings are typically the driest of all. They also are the most full bodied and highest in alcohol. These Rieslings should be reserved for heavier fare, while the Germans match better with lighter fare. Great with any pork, chicken, or duck dish.

Gewurztraminer
Originally from Italy, this white grape is gaining popularity. The word "gewurz" is German for spicy and that is exactly what kind of wine this grape can produce. Gewurztraminer is fuller in body than Rieslings and is very floral with dense hints of peach. Great with any heavier pork, chicken, or duck dish.

Pinot Gris
Completely different style of wine than the Pinot Grigio of Northern Italy. Here, in Alsace, Pinot Gris is rich, fat, and honeyed. Luscious hints of pear and apple are supported and balanced by high acidity and a minerally touch. Great with foie gras. This grape may also be called Tokay D'Alsace, which is not to be confused with Italy's Tocai Friulano or Hungary's Tokaji Aszù.

Pinot Blanc
Not as creamy and spicy like Pinot Gris. More subtle hints of apple and spice. High acidity makes this a very food friendly wine.

Sparkling

Cremant D'Alsace
A great non-Champagne alternative. Made from **Pinot Gris, Pinot Blanc, Riesling, and Pinot Noir**. These dry sparklers are great with shellfish, fish, and many different appetizers. Hard to find but definitely worth the search.

CENTRAL WEST

BORDEAUX

Bordeaux is broken up into 5 main districts:

Pomerol
Saint Emilion
Médoc
Graves
Sauternes

POMEROL

Pomerol is the smallest of the five main districts. Its wines are made primarily with the red grape called **Merlot**. Small amounts of **Cabernet Sauvignon and Cabernet Franc** are added; however, these two grapes are usually softer and less tannic than in other parts of Bordeaux. Pomerol wines are pretty big and rich, considering it is made from Merlot, a grape known mostly for its softness. Good Pomerols usually exhibit hints of earth, blackberries, dark chocolate, nuts, and licorice. Good Pomerols are also expensive. Great with lamb dishes. Pomerol whites, along with other Bordeaux whites in general, are never really significant.

SAINT EMILION

Saint Emilion is considered to be the second best of Bordeaux, the first being Médoc. Made primarily from **Merlot** grapes and occasionally blended with **Cabernet Franc and Cabernet Sauvignon**. Typically softer and easier drinking than other Bordeaux wines. They are less tannic and higher in alcohol. Unlike New World Merlot based wines, Saint Emilion wines can mirror Pomerol, with its earthiness and softness. Also ideal with lamb dishes. Its whites are never really significant.

MÉDOC

Médoc is broken up into 4 main areas:

Margaux, Pauillac
Saint Estèphe, Saint Julien

Margaux

One of the best in the Bordeaux region. Margaux wines are made primarily from **Cabernet Sauvignon** grapes. **Cabernet Franc, Merlot, and Petit Verdot** are also blended in the wine. These are some of the legendary Bordeaux wines that can age for a very long time. Margaux wines are known to be very elegant with an incredibly balanced and perfumed bouquet. These Cabernet based wines differ from New World Cabernets in the sense that they hold back on overemphasizing the fruit. Margaux wines tend to be earthier and are much better suited for meals than 90% of New World wines. Great with red meats and many other "artery-clogging" foods.

Pauillac

The biggest and roughest of the Bordeaux wines, Pauillacs are meant to age very long. Huge body with very firm structure. Made from **Cabernet Sauvignon** grapes and may be blended with smaller amounts of **Cabernet Franc, Merlot, Malbec, and Petit Verdot**. These wines can be beasts, so pair them with some serious fare.

Saint Estèphe

The most tannic and age worthy wine of Bordeaux. Typically not as good as the other Bordeaux wines. Primarily made from **Cabernet Sauvignon** with smaller amounts of **Merlot, Cabernet Franc and Petit Verdot**. Today, producers are using more Merlot to help soften these austere wines. The average ones are quite pricey and good ones are even pricier.

Saint Julien

The smallest communes in Médoc. **Cabernet Sauvignon** is the dominant grape with **Cabernet Franc, Merlot, and Petit Verdot** used in small amounts. Some believe Saint Julien wines to be some of the best in the World. Sometimes, they are right. Saint Julien is also very pricey. Age worthy and very elegant. Great with red meat.

GRAVES

Graves wines are made primarily from **Cabernet Sauvignon** grapes. Smaller amounts of **Merlot and Cabernet Franc** are blended. Graves reds can be very similar to those in Médoc but typically softer than Médoc wines, due to the higher percentage of Merlot. Graves wines are great ageing wines and have that characteristic earthiness so prevalent in Bordeaux wines. A great choice for grilled meats. **Pessac-Léognan** is a sub region of Graves that makes terrific reds and Bordeaux's best **white wine**, made mostly from **Sauvignon Blanc**, with smaller amounts of **Semillon and Muscadelle**.

SAUTERNES

THE dessert wine of France. Known worldwide, Sauternes wines demand high prices. **Semillon** is a white grape and the main one used, however, tiny amounts of **Sauvignon Blanc and Muscadelle** may be added. Good Sauternes have golden hints of almonds, honey, peach, apricots, pineapple, and even coconut, all presented as a creamy, rich, and textured masterpiece. Great accompaniment to blue cheeses or foie gras.

COGNAC

The town Cognac is world renown for producing the famous brandy with the same name. Brandy is essentially liquor that is distilled from wine and then aged in wood. Brandy may be made using other fruits. An example is Calvados, made from apples. Given this is a book about wines made from grapes, then Cognac will be discussed and Calvados will not. Cognac is made primarily from the white **Trebbiano** grape (in France called **Ugni Blanc**). After fermentation, the wine is distilled twice. It is then placed in Limousin wood casks to age and mellow its sharp and harsh taste.

Stars on the label imply that the wine has been aged. The more stars, the more ageing, and, therefore, the higher the quality.

You will see these terms on the **older** Cognac bottle's label:
V.S. (Very Superior)
V.S.O.P. (Very Superior Old Pale)
V.V.S.O.P. (Very, Very Superior Old Pale)

The label terms:
X.O., Extra, and Reserve usually mean that the Cognac is the oldest one put out by the producer.

The label term **Fine Champagne** means that at least 60% of the grapes come from the better vineyards of Cognac, called **Grande Champagne**.
If it says **Grande Fine Champagne**, all the grapes come from that area.
DO NOT CONFUSE this with Champagne, the northeast region which produces sparkling wine.

CENTRAL EAST

BURGUNDY

Burgundy has 5 main regions:

Chablis
Côte D'Or
Côte Chalonnaise
Mâconnais
Beaujolais

CHABLIS
Chablis makes white wine using the **Chardonnay** grape. Chablis is considered, by the smart people, to be Burgundy's best white. Oaked little, if any, Chablis whites are very high in acidity and boast its characteristic lemony notes. They have a flinty and mineral quality. The cool climate prevents the grapes from ripening too much, so the acidity stays high. This allows Chablis to be perfectly food friendly. Great with shellfish, fish, and white meats.

CÔTE D'OR
Côte D'Or is divided into 2 parts:
Côte de Nuits and **Côte de Beaune**

Both produce fabulous red and white wines, however,
Côte de Nuits is famous for its red wines while Côte de Beaune is famous for its whites.

Côte de Nuits
World famous for its **Pinot Noir**. Considered to be possibly the best Pinot Noir wine in the world. Côte de Nuits has numerous villages, which are famous for their wines and even carry the villages' name on the label. The better-known villages are **Vosne-Romanée, Gevrey-Chambertin, Nuits Saint-George, and Vougeout**, among others. The medium bodied reds from here are high in acidity with spicy, cherry notes. Here, Pinot Noir offers hints of earthiness. Great with hams and creamier cheeses such as Brie.

Côte de Beaune
World Famous for its **Chardonnay**. Considered to be the best Chardonnay wine in the world. Côte de Beaune also has numerous villages that are famous for their wines and even carry the villages' name on the label. The better-known ones are **Meursault, Chassagne-Montrachet, Puligny-Montrachet, Savigny-Lès-Beaune, Aloxe Corton, and Auxey-Duresses**, among others. These Chardonnay based wines are typically medium bodied. In Meursault, the wines are nuttier and butterier. In Montrachet, the wines can be more concentrated and smoky. Côte de Beaune whites can be and usually are the most expensive whites in the world. **Pommard** and **Volnay** are basically the two villages that produce the best **Pinot Noir** in the Côte de Beaune. Pommard can even be quite full bodied, considering it is made from Pinot Noir.

CÔTE CHALONNAISE
Côte Chalonnaise produces both red from **Pinot Noir** and white from **Chardonnay**. Not considered as good as other Burgundy whites. New producers are creating better wines but, as a whole, these wines are nothing crazy.

MÂCONNAIS

The Mâconnais is well known for its white wine made from **Chardonnay**. It is typically lighter bodied than most other Chardonnays and fermented in stainless steel tanks. Mâconnais whites are crisp and minerally. Cheaper and actually better than Côte Chalonnaise. A great, inexpensive example would be **Mâcon-Villages**. Should be drunk as early as possible. **Saint Véran** is also a good value wine from this area, too. **Pouilly Fuissé** is the most famous appellation and produces some of the better whites of the Mâconnais.

BEAUJOLAIS

The most southern part of the Burgundy region. It differs from the rest of Burgundy because it makes wine made from the red grape **Gamay**. These wines are known to have hints of raspberries, cherries, and black pepper. It has very little tannins and little alcohol but its acidity level is pretty good. All Beaujolais wines should be drunk young. **Beaujolais Nouveau** should be drunk immediately after production. Beaujolais Nouveau (new in French) is wine made toward the end of every year. The Gamay grapes are pressed and bottled immediately. It is a fresh young wine that is released every third week of November and should be drunk until January.

SOUTHWEST

CAHORS

This area produces what will forever be referred to as "black wines". This is because the wines produced primarily from **Malbec** grapes are very dark, tannic, and need time to age. Malbec is usually used for blending in Bordeaux, but here it is a shining star. It exhibits dark flavors of raisins and tobacco. Makes a great accompaniment to steak. It is like the Guinness of wine, an acquired taste. So, hurry up and acquire!

MADIRAN

If Cahors is an acquired taste, then I do not know what to say about Madiran. **Tannat** is the dominant grape. It is red and produces very big, dark, tannic, and rough wines. So big and rough, in fact, that big grapes, like Cabernet, are used to soften Tannat up! These wines need time to age and, even then, should only be paired with red meat.

ARMAGNAC

Armagnac is a region that makes very fine brandy under the same name. Armagnac is considered one of the world's best brandies, second only to Cognac. Armagnac is distilled only once, whereas Cognac is distilled twice. If brandy is distilled less, it is left with more pronounced flavors. Armagnac is also aged in wood. The wood, called Black Oak, gives more flavor than Cognac's Limousin Oak. The Black Oak also speeds up the ageing process. Usually fuller than Cognac, Armagnac lack's Cognac's finesse.

SOUTHEAST

RHÔNE

The Rhône region has many wines and wine growing areas. **The main ones** to know are:

**Côtes du Rhône, Rasteau, Côte-Rôtie
Condrieu, Hermitage
Crozes- Hermitage, Cornas
Vacqueyras, Gigondas
Châteauneuf-du-Pape, Tavel
Beaumes de Venise**

Côtes du Rhône
This is the general term applied to red, white, and rosé wines produced in the Rhône region. These wines are typically inexpensive and blend **Syrah, Grenache, Cinsault, and Mourvèdre** for the reds, while using **Marsanne, Roussanne, and Grenache Blanc** grapes for the whites. The whites are usually overshadowed by the reds, which can be very good and prices are never too high. Red Côtes du Rhône can be light bodied, medium, or even full bodied. Either one, these wines will always have spicy and peppery hints with soft red and black fruits. These characteristics come from the Syrah and Mourvèdre grapes. Meant to be drunk earlier than other Rhône wines. Good with chicken dishes, lamb dishes, and even tacos, or pizza.

Rasteau
This area is known for their sweet wines, but they make great, dry reds from **Grenache, Syrah, and Mourvédre**.

Côte-Rôtie
The most northern part of the Rhône region. Côte-Rôtie produces only red wines made from **Syrah** and a maximum of 20% of white **Viognier** grapes. The Syrah lends the spiciness and peppery traits, while the white Viognier offers the big exotic aromas. Côte-Rôtie has notes of blackberries, raspberries, and cassis with a hint of smokiness. One of the more elegant of the Rhône wines. These rich and full bodied wines can be some of the best in the world. Côte-Rôtie can and should age for quite a while. Beautifully paired with grilled meats, especially those with heavy sauces.

Condrieu
Condrieu makes only white wine made from the **Viognier** grape. Viognier is very aromatic. It has strong notes of apricots, peaches, honey, and spice. Acidity, unfortunately, can be quite low. Very little is produced, so it is hard to find and pretty expensive. Great with spicy cuisines and a natural pair with pork and chicken.

Hermitage
Hermitage is well known for its reds and whites, but the reds are what leave people dreaming. Made primarily from **Syrah** with occasional blends of a little white **Marsanne and Roussanne** grapes. Hermitage wines are very big, robust, and powerful. They are meant to age. These wines are tannic and full bodied with notes of tar. Not as elegant as Côte-Rôtie. Amazing stuff and obviously expensive. Great with heavy fare. Again, RED meat.

Crozes-Hermitage

These wines are very similar to Hermitage, although usually not as good. Softer and less intense than Hermitage. Good but you can get Hermitage for the same price or maybe a little more.

Cornas

Increasingly becoming more popular, Cornas makes only red wines primarily from the **Syrah** grape. The wines can be some of the biggest and most tannic in all of Rhône. Although hard to find, Cornas is worth it. Many believe Cornas will only get better and, soon, wine drinkers everywhere will direct their attention to this place.

Vacqueyras

The majority of each bottling is **Grenache**, with **Syrah and Mourvèdre** filling out the rest.

Gigondas

Made primarily from **Grenache** grapes. Sometimes blended with **Syrah, Cinsault, and Mourvèdre**. Big wines with high levels of alcohol. Gigondas has dark fruits and benefits from a few years of ageing.

Châteauneuf-du-Pape

Either THE best or, at least, tied with Côte-Rôtie for the number one spot in Rhône. Châteauneuf-du-Pape makes very little white. The reds are so good that nobody ever cares about the whites. The dominant red grape is **Grenache**. It is usually blended with smaller amounts of **Syrah, Cinsault, and Mourvèdre**, among others. Châteauneuf-du-Pape wines are easily recognizable by the imprinted, papal coat of arms logo on the bottle, given the (then) Pope temporarily moved the Papacy to Avignon in the 1300's, for about 70 years. These wines are huge and earthy, with full flavors of raspberries, black berries, black currants, and herbs. Good Châteauneuf-du-Pape can be expensive but if any wine is worth the extra cash, it is THIS. It's one of my father's top 3, maybe # 1, favorite wines. Excellent with red meats.

Tavel

This area makes only **rosé** wine. These rosés are fuller and drier. Made primarily from **Grenache and Cinsault**. Considered one of the world's best rosé wines.

Beaumes de Venise

This area makes great dry reds but the focus is on their dessert wines called **Muscat de Beaumes de Venise**.

PROVENCE

There are 2 main areas:
Bandol, Coteaux d'Aix en Provence

Bandol

Better known for its red wines made from **Mourvèdre**. **Rosés** are made from **Grenache, Syrah, and Cinsault**. Good value wine that are worth the search.

Coteaux d'Aix en Provence

Great reds and rosés from **Cabernet Sauvignon, Cinsault, Grenache, Syrah, and Mourvèdre**. Incredible value among too many overpriced and over-marketed French wines. Find some.

LANGUEDOC-ROUSSILLON

There are many wines and wine areas. The ones you should know are:

Corbières, Faugères
Fitou, Minervois
Saint-Chinian, Picpoul de Pinet
Rivesaltes

Corbières
Produces wine primarily from **Carignan**. High in alcohol and tannins and quite spicy.

Faugères
These reds are good to very good on average. They are made primarily from Rhône varieties such as **Grenache, Syrah, Carignan, Cinsault, and Mourvèdre**. Getting better year by year and is worth a try.

Fitou
Possibly the best of this region. Made from **Carignan, Cinsault, Grenache, Syrah, and Mourvèdre**. Great with the famous bean dishes of this area.

Minervois
Full-bodied red made with **Carignan and Grenache**. Getting better every year especially with larger additions of **Syrah and Mourvèdre**.

Saint-Chinian
Along with Faugères and Fitou, Saint-Chinian takes its place as one of the best southern French reds. Saint-Chinian uses **Carignan and Grenache** with steadily increasing percentages of **Syrah and Mourvèdre**. Spicy and slightly herbal, these wines can be a little hard to find.

Picpoul de Pinet
Picpoul means "sting the lips" in French and this zesty, lemony juice from the grape, Picpoul, is usually used for its high acidity in Rhône blends but does well on its own in Languedoc-Roussillon. It's great with seafood or for sipping with appetizers.

Rivesaltes
Rivesaltes is known for making sweet, fortified wines. The winemaking approach is called **ambré**, which allows the wine to be oxidized, giving it its characteristic nutty flavor. The other positive of it being already oxidized is that, once opened, it can stay and be drinkable for months after. Rivesaltes can be made from white **Muscat** or white **Macabeu** or from red **Grenache** grapes.

ISLAND

CORSICA

Until a few hundred years ago, the beautiful island of Corsica was Italian. In fact, Napoleon, who was originally Italian, was born in almost the exact period the island was conquered by France. The wines are more Italian than French and their white wines are made from **Vermentinu or Rolle**, which is actually the Italian Vermentino. Their reds are mostly made from **Nielluccio**, which is really the Italian Sangiovese. The island makes a lot of Rosé wines, made from **Nielluccio (Sangiovese) and Sciacarello**, which may be related to Italy's Mammolo and Pollera Nera.

GEORGIA

Most are only familiar with Georgia, the U.S. state, but the country of Georgia is a very old one and one of the oldest wine producing countries in the world. **The main wine region** is **Kakheti** and has many sub-regions. Most of Georgian wines are stored in **Kvevri earthenware vessels** placed into the ground.

The main red grape is called **Saperavi** and it makes deep, dark, age-worthy wines. **Rkatsiteli** is the main white grape and is usually made into **orange wines**, where the white grape juice is left in contact with the pulp, skins, and seeds longer than it normally would to give the wine an orange color and deeper flavor profile.

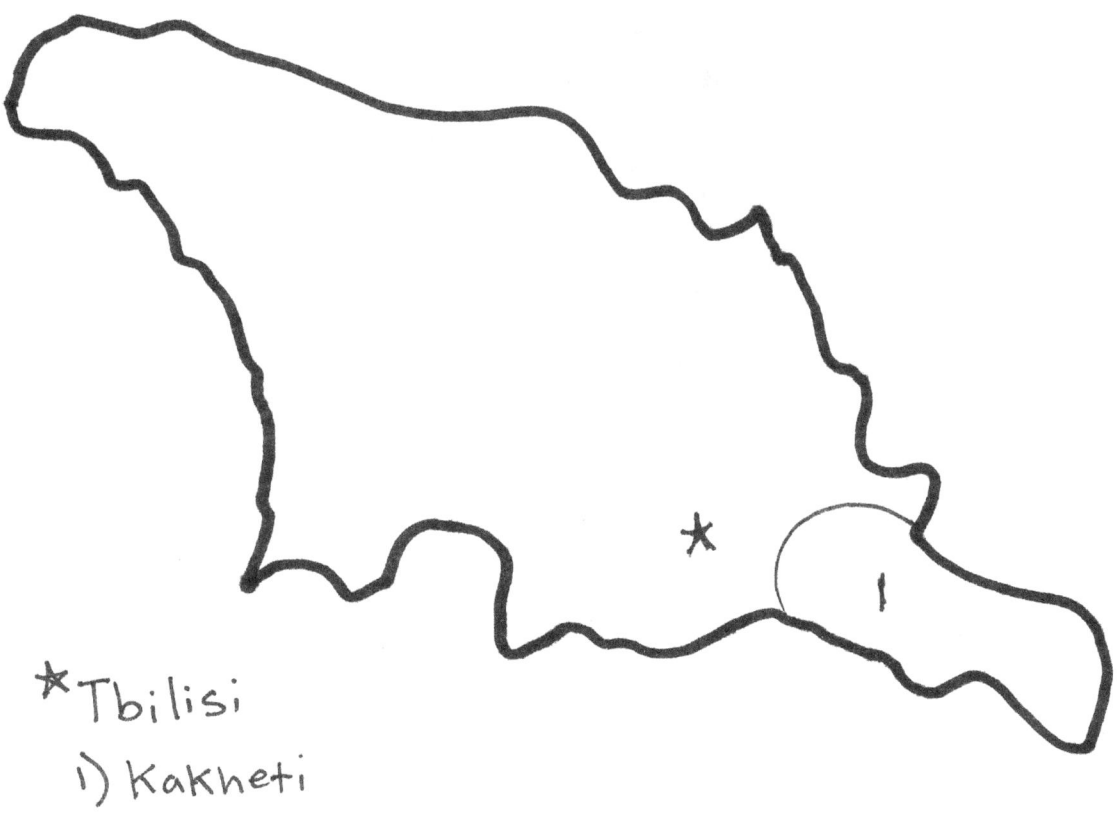

*Tbilisi
1) Kakheti

GEORGIA

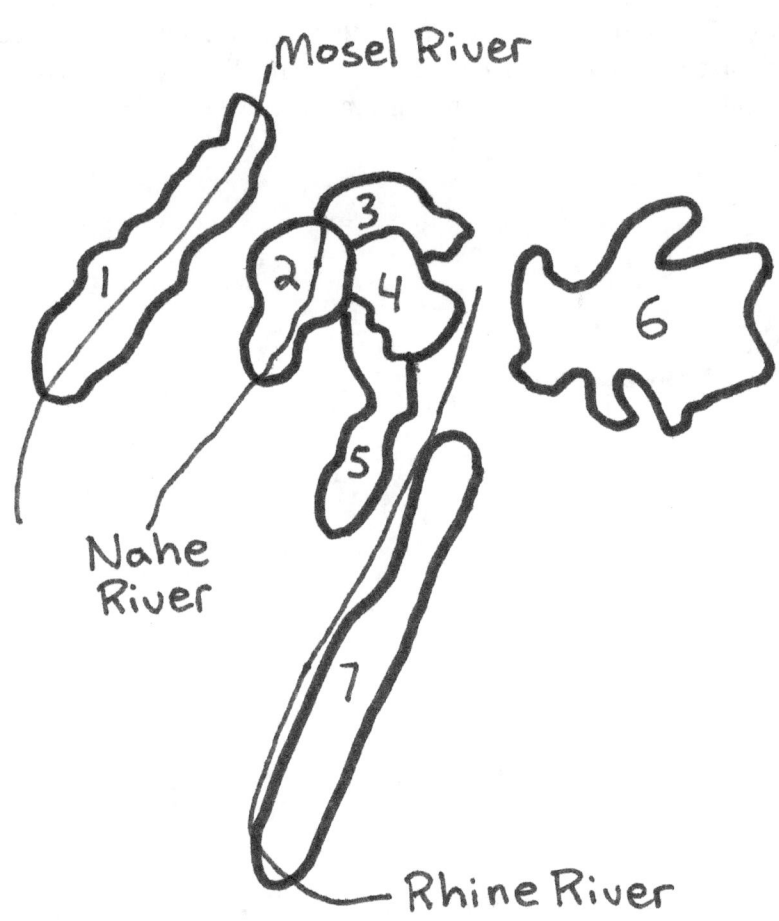
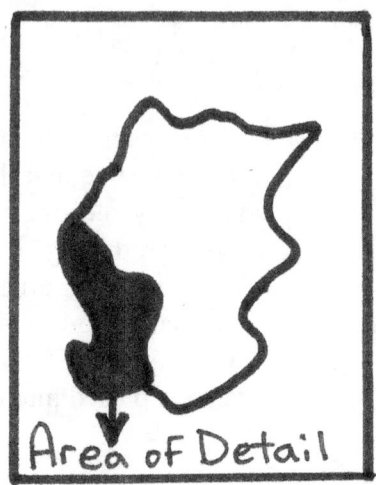

1) Mosel-Saar-Ruwer
2) Nahe
3) Rheingau
4) Rheinhessen
5) Rheinpfalz
6) Franken
7) Baden

GERMANY

GERMANY

What is it that people do not get about German wines? Excuse me, what is it about *most* people? Germany, unfortunately, is typically overlooked and ignored in wine conversations. That is, in conversations with wine novices. Before I continue, I must acknowledge a man who has helped shape the minds of many wine lovers. This man is considered by many a radical, crazy, a nut job, etc. I heard it all. But you know what? He is about 99% accurate on his opinion and understanding of wine. His name is Willie Gluckstern. He is a wine author, a wine teacher, and, of course, a wine importer. The wine world was waiting for someone like him. Throughout the book, I took careful attention not to mention a producer's name or even certain brands. With this one, however, I feel it is a duty to talk.

Willie Gluckstern helped me along with countless others see the wonderful world of German wines. He more importantly helped unravel the lies, myths, and misunderstandings of so many of today's popular New World, New Style wines. His book is called "The Wine Avenger." If anything, I propose you buy his book over mine. I also highly suggest you enroll in his wine classes. Even better, I strongly suggest you discover his wines. Do these three things and I guarantee you will be better off.

Ok, back to business. Germany has been blessed with the capability to claim the number one spot for both the white grape Riesling and the wines it produces. Nowhere in the world can this grape prosper as well as in Germany. Nowhere in the world is there white wine so unique and *SO* good! I allow people to have their own opinions, BUT LISTEN UP! Riesling *is* the world's best white wine grape. Like it or not. If you don't agree, it is because you do not get it. Say anything about anything, but please hear me out on this one.

Riesling is genetically superior to almost any grape out there (FACT). People often mistake Rieslings as sweet wines. Oaked California Chardonnays are sweet wines. The oak gives off a vanilla creamy sweetness. Those Chardonnays are sweet. Rieslings, on the other hand, have a very high level of sugar. I compare the Riesling grape to very good fruit, like a banana that is naturally high in sugars. The sugars in Riesling are perfectly balanced by its high level of acidity. Almost always, the sugar/acidity situation is a give and take. If you increase one, you will lose the other. This is not so with Riesling. It incredibly has high levels of both. More sugars mean more flavor and more acidity means it is more food friendly (FACT). Rieslings can be paired with more different foods than any other grape, white or red (FACT). This is why Riesling is superior.

I always said that two completely different people with opposing, extreme views usually end up doing and liking the same things for exactly different reasons. Riesling is a perfect example of this. Only wine novices or wine connoisseurs like or even love Riesling. No one in the middle does. When someone first starts drinking wine, they want something sweet and pleasant. The more that person delves into wine, they start to seek drier wines and wrongly think Riesling is on the same level as a cheap, wine cooler. It is only when that person advances to the third step that Riesling is viewed for what it is : an incredible grape with high acidity and sugar but perfectly balanced. This example of two different people can be applied to other aspects of Life.

Thank God not too many people realize this because you can get great Rieslings for relatively cheap. On top of all this, Rieslings from Germany are low in alcohol, which makes it automatically more versatile. It is also possibly the grape that best expresses its terroir. Rieslings are so great that blending another grape in its wines could actually ruin it. It can stand all alone and be as pretty as it wants. In fact, Rieslings are blended in other boring wines to liven them up. In Alsace, France, and in Austria, the Rieslings are bigger, earthier, and drier. In Germany they are lighter and have the least alcohol. German Rieslings are the most elegant whites around.

Germany's cool weather climate and soil types are perfect for making great white wine. The best vineyards are along the Mosel and Rhine rivers. The grapes are planted on slopes so steep (a good thing) that harvesting is usually done manually rather than mechanically. Other grapes that do well in Germany are Gewurztraminer, Muller Thurgau, Sylvaner, and Scheurebe. It is believed that these grapes play a lesser role in representing Germany's best wines.

VERY IMPORTANT!!!

When buying German Rieslings, you should take notice of certain words on the label. The German labels are very informative. Written on the labels are descriptions of ripeness. These words will tell you the level of ripeness, meaning when the grapes were picked and, therefore, the sweetness, acidity, and body of the wine.

The levels of ripeness are:

Kabinett: Dry, light to medium body, elegant, highest acidity with moderate sweetness.

Spatlese: The grapes are picked later, so the grapes have a higher level of sugar. They are fuller bodied and fruitier.

Auslese: Very ripe. Medium bodied and a much higher level of sugar than the previous two.

Beerenauslese: Picked from a selected bunch of very ripened grapes (almost shriveled). Sweet enough to be considered dessert wines.

Trockenbeerenauslese: Picked even later. The grapes are very sweet.

Eiswein (Ice Wine): As the name implies, the grapes are picked frozen. Most of the grapes' content is solid with very little liquid, all of which is extremely concentrated. The grapes are left to hang and are not picked usually until January. The sweetest of all. Only grapes like Riesling can produce such sweet wines and make them feel light in the mouth. The lightness comes from the grape's high acidity. This balance of sugar and acidity is unparalleled in any other grape.

Please Note:

Kabinett and Spatlese Rieslings may sometimes be divided into 2 categories:

Trocken: means dry, almost no residual sugar.

Halbtrocken: means half dry. Still pretty dry, but a little more body and fruit.

Germany has many wine regions.
The major 7 all lie along or between the rivers Mosel and Rhine and are:

Mosel, Nahe, Rheinhessen, Rheingau, Rheinpfalz, Franken, Baden

MOSEL

Mosel wines come in long, skinny, *green* bottles. They are the wines with the lowest alcohol (7.5 – 10%) in Germany. The Mosel makes great **Rieslings** that are very delicate and elegant. These flowery wines display hints of the typical fruits of the fall season. Soft hints of apples, citrus, pears, and, of course slate, (from the soil the vines grow in). Great with so many foods, the list would be endless. Try it with light fish or shellfish.

The Mosel river has 2 tributaries:
Saar and Ruwer.
These two both produce great Rieslings.

The **Saar Rieslings** come from a higher altitude and have higher acidity and, therefore, can age longer.

The **Ruwer Rieslings** are the more delicate, elegant, and smooth of the two.

NAHE

The Nahe is a river that actually lies in between the Mosel and the Rhine. The **Riesling** wines take on traits of both surrounding wine regions. The wines are very minerally, stony, and very aromatic. It has the elegance of Mosel wines with the heavier body of the Rhine wines. Nahe wines are great, if you can find them. Perfect accompaniment to many fish dishes, shellfish, as well as appetizers and snacks.

RHINE

Rheinhessen, Rheingau, and Rheinpfalz are all wine regions associated with the Rhine river. All three have similarities that define Rhine wines.

Rhine wines come in long, skinny, *brown* bottles. They have a slightly higher level of alcohol (9 – 10%). The Rhine makes mostly **Rieslings** that are a little heavier in body, although still quite light and very elegant. These wines typically exhibit hints of summer fruits such as peaches, apricots, currants, and berries. Again, great with many different foods.

RHEINHESSEN

This wine region is located Northwest of the Rhine. It produces mostly **Rieslings**, which are softer than those from neighboring areas. These wines typically have smoky hints, with notes of roasted summer fruits. These wines are a steal and some of the best value wines in Germany, and the world for that matter. This region is also a big producer of white wines made from **Sylvaner** that are soft, light, and earthy with pretty good acidity. Can even display nice hints of smokiness and grapefruit. This region also makes wine from the white grape **Scheurebe**, which is a cross between Rieslings and Sylvaner and displays characteristics of both.

RHEINGAU

This region lies Northeast of the Rhine. It produces mostly **Rieslings** and is best known specifically for its Kabinetts. The Rieslings here are bigger and drier than most of the other German ones. They are richer and more full-bodied with long ageing capabilities. Many top wine estates can be found here in Rheingau.

RHEINPFALZ (PFALZ)

This is Germany's warmest and driest wine region. Produces less Riesling wines than other German wine regions. The warm weather produces **Riesling**s that are full bodied, richer, and with a higher level of alcohol. Rheinpfalz is better known for its **Gewurztraminer** wines. Gewurztraminer is derived from the German word "gewurz" which means spicy. Typically, these wines are spicy with hints of flowers, in particular rose petals. They are fuller bodied than Rieslings. Here, Gewurztraminers are lighter than the ones from nearby Alsace and Austria. The German Gewurztraminer is fruitier, lighter, and lower in alcohol, with good acidity and medium sweetness.

FRANKEN

The cold weather of Franken is better suited for grapes such as **Muller Thurgau and Sylvaner**. Sylvaners from Franken are considered some of the best in the country. They typically display the earthiness so prevalent in all Franken wines. Sylvaner here is at its biggest and richest. They are also some of Germany's driest wines. Sugar levels are pretty low.

BADEN

The southernmost wine region in Germany. Known specifically for its **Pinot Noir, called Spatburgunder** in Germany. The acidity is typically not as high as compared to other wines from neighboring regions. The Pinot Noirs can be very elegant, with bright cherry and strawberry fruit. Unbelievably food friendly, but also very hard to find.

★ Athens
1) Macedonia
2) Attica
3) Peloponnese
4) Santorini
5) Samos
6) Cyprus

GREECE

GREECE

Wine has long played an important role in Greek life. Myths and stories describe the wines of Ancient Greece to have been quite good but, up until the 1990's, Greek wines unfortunately did not support this belief. For a long time, Greek producers have made less than mediocre wine and the Greek consumer kept his/her mouth shut. No one complained, so no improvements were made.

There has been some good news coming. People woke up. Producers are eliminating old techniques, which have proven ineffective. They now have adopted a newer approach, but always keeping it rustic and traditional, which is the right thing to do. As usual, international varieties are also big here but the wines made from the indigenous grapes are the ones that are gaining interest. When the wines are made correctly, they can be good at affordable prices. As always, Greek wine goes best with great, Greek food.

There are many wine regions in Greece. **The main ones** to know are:

Peloponnese
Attica
Cyprus
Macedonia
Santorini
Samos

PELOPONNESE

The 3 main areas of Peloponnese to know are: **Nemea, Patras, Mantinia**

NEMEA
Some of the best red wine of Greece comes from this area. The dominant red grape is **Agiorgitiko (St. George)**. This grape can produce big, spicy wines with hints of plums and dark fruits. It has pretty low acidity, unless it is grown at higher altitudes. Also makes some pretty good rosé wine. Great wine for lamb dishes.

PATRAS

Mavrodaphne
A red grape that produces good dessert wine. The best come from in and around a town named **Patras**. This wine is full bodied and very aromatic. Ageing in oak barrels softens the wine. Mavrodaphne should be served at room temperature, not cold.

Muscat
Sweet and aromatic with big apricot scents. **Peloponnese** produces most of the better Muscats in Greece.

MANTINIA

Moscophilero
A good white Greek grape. It is typically added to wines to give character. It is considered to have both characteristics of Gewurztraminer and Muscat. It actually might have even higher acidity than both. It can be made as a white or even rosé.

ATTICA

Whites
Retsina, Savatiano, Roditis

Rosé
Roditis

Whites

Retsina
Retsina is made all over Greece, but in Attica they are particularly popular. Retsina can be any wine that has been flavored with pine resin. It is considered an acquired taste to non-Greeks. The usual grapes used to make Retsina are **Savatiano, Roditis, and Assyrtiko**. Hard to find outside of Greece.

Savatiano
The most planted grape in Greece is never anything special. It is typically used to make **Retsina** wine. On its own, it is average with low acidity and slight hints of oranges. There are very good, age-worth exceptions, though, you should definitely seek out.

Rosé

Roditis
Can be quite average. The better, pink-skinned varieties are usually added to increase quality and add complexity. Good acidity and should be drunk young. Enjoy with shellfish.

CYPRUS

Dessert
Commandaria

Commandaria
Made from the red grape **Mavro**, Commandaria can resemble Spanish Sherries. Good Commandaria is hard to find, but definitely worth it.

MACEDONIA

Reds
Xynomavro

Xynomavro
A very dark colored red grape that produces full bodied wines. It is very high in acidity and tannins. These wines are rich and spicy. One of the top reds of Greece. They are capable of ageing quite a while and are best suited for heavy fare. For now, the best wines of this region come from an area called **Naoussa**.

SANTORINI

Whites
Santorini

Dessert
Vino Santo

Whites

Santorini
The dry white wines of this region are labeled Santorini. Made from the white grape named **Assyrtiko**. If not oaked, these wines can be some of the best of Greece and happen to be one of my favorite white wines in the World. It has high acidity and is stony and minerally. Age-worthy. A food friendly wine that is perfect with fish and shellfish.

Dessert

Vino Santo
Greece's version of Italian Vin Santo. The **Assyrtiko** grape is used and the hot weather boosts the sugar levels. As a result, alcohol is usually quite high (15%). The grapes are dried in the hot sun, pressed, and the wine is then aged. The result is an Oloroso-like Sherry.

SAMOS

After Dinner
Metaxa (Brandy)

Dessert
Muscat

After Dinner

Metaxa
Greece's most famous brandy. Made primarily from the neutral, white grape **Savatiano**. Muscat is usually blended to add sweetness and life to the brandy. The brandy is aged in oak for more developed flavors and aromas.

Dessert

Muscat
If made well, Samos Muscats can be some of the best values in the category of dessert wines. There is a big demand for these wines from this island. They typically have hints of apricots, peaches, and even citrus. Look hard for these wines, because they can be good for little money.

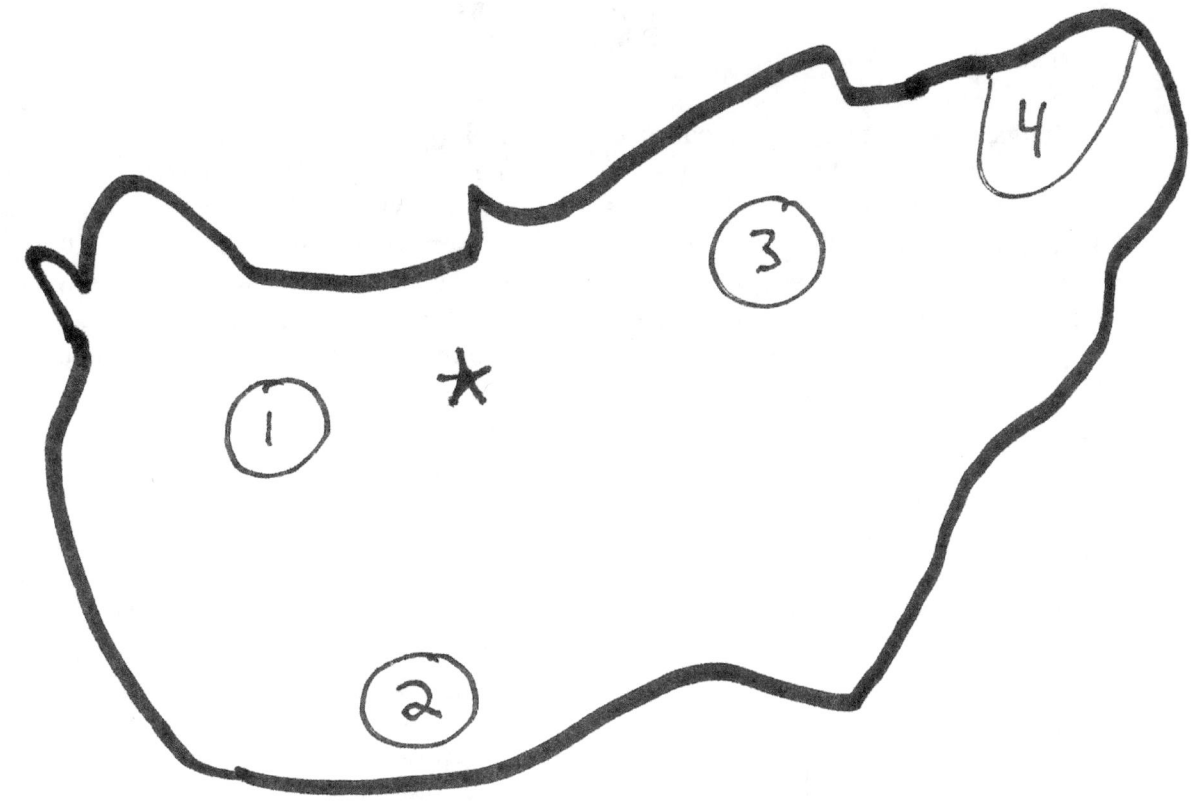

★ Budapest
1) Nagy Samló
2) Villány
3) Eger
4) Tokaj

HUNGARY

HUNGARY

Hungarians are nice people but have had it rough for quite a bit. Besides having their rich history and progress stopped due to communism, their once thriving wine industry was completely wiped out from pests. The good news is the resilience of the people is coming through and the wine industry is open for business once again.

There are **4 main wine regions** : **Eger, Tokaj, Villány, Nagy Somló**

The best 2 are **Eger and Tokaj**.

Eger
Eger is must famous for its **Egri Bikavér** blend. It translates to bull's blood and it's made from **Kékfrankos**, which is actually the German grape, **Blaufrankish**, and blended with other varietals like **Cabernet Sauvignon and Cabernet Franc**.

Tokaj
Tokaj is known for its dessert wines and for dry whites. The most famous of the dessert wines is the **Tokaji Aszú**. It's one of the best dessert wines in the world. Incredible. As incredible, is the fact that producers of this wine area, famous for dessert wines made from local, Hungarian grapes, won a court battle in the European Union against Italy's producers of Tocai Friulano, an Italian and totally different grape. Friuli, Italy is no longer allowed to sell their wines from Tocai Friulano grapes and label them such because of Hungary's Tokaji Aszú dessert wines from the Tokaj wine region, made from completely different grapes. When made dry, Tokaj whites, from **Furmint** grapes make wines that taste like a cross between Gruner Veltliner and Riesling.

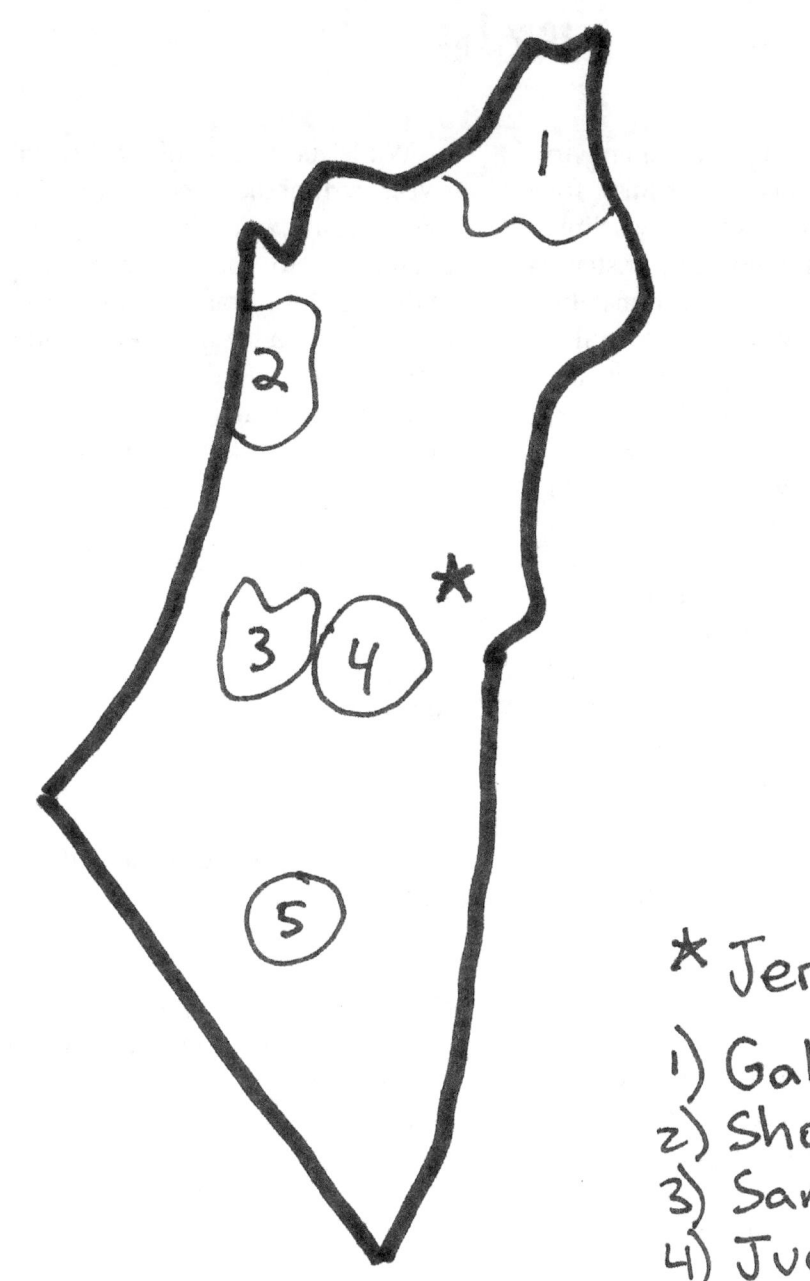

ISRAEL

ISRAEL

The Holy Land has been home to Jews, Christians, and Muslims for thousands of years. While Muslims abstain from alcohol, Jews and Christians do drink wine. In Israel, unfortunately, wine quality was never high up until a few years ago. Perhaps, when the Romans governed the land, it was good but it definitely took a fall since then. Until about the year 2000, quality Israeli wine was almost impossible to find. Things have been changing. Whether you believe or not, the Bible is filled with references to wine and its important and holy symbolism. Jesus Christ turned water into wine and even offered it as "His Blood", the new Covenant. In modern day Israel, consumption is low but winemakers there are attempting to change that. With modern technology and experts from France, Italy, and California there to help and teach age-old techniques, and modern ones, too, there is promise in the Holy Land.

Not all wines in Israel are Kosher, but most do receive that certification. The grapes are kosher but it depends on who comes into contact with the wine to make it kosher. Only Sabbath-observing Jews are allowed to be involved in the winemaking process in order for it to be strictly kosher. If the wines are boiled, they are labeled "Mevushal" and then can be handled by non-Sabbath observing Jews and still be kosher. Needless to say, boiling wine ruins it and makes it taste something awful. To minimize the damage, flash pasteurization can be done, but the results are still dismal. If the wine is not mevushal, it must be opened and served only by Sabbath-observing Jews in order to still be considered Kosher.

While most think of Kosher wines as sweet, red, grape juice with alcohol, the many kosher wines now being made are attempting to change that view and reality. All the grapes of any importance are all international varieties, originally from France. Red wines make up the overwhelming majority of the country's production. Israeli wines tend to be New World in style.

Israel has **5 main wine growing regions**.

Galil (Galilee)
Shomron
Samson
Judean Hills
Negev

The best two are Galil and the Judean Hills.

Galil
Galil (A.K.A. Galilee) includes the **Golan Heights, Upper Galilee, and the Lower Galilee.** This area has been hotly contested since the 1967 "Six-day War". It used to be part of Syria, but then became part of Israel. It became official for Israel in the early 1980's but many countries across the World refuse to accept this area as part of Israel. In fact, the wines from this area are sometimes not allowed to be sold as Israeli. The tension is unfortunate, given this is where Christ performed two famous Miracles : turning water into wine at the wedding at Cana and walked on water on the Sea of Galilee. Hopefully, we can expect another miracle for the current and problematic situation. Galil's best sub-region is the Golan Heights and it is also the best in the country. Its high altitudes

and cool breezes are ideal for wine grape growing. **Cabernet, Merlot, Syrah, Grenache, Carginan, and Mourvèdre** do well here. **Chardonnay** is made here, too, but usually too New World in style.

Shomron
Shomron is also called **Samaria**. We have all heard the famous Bible parable of the Good Samaritan. The wines are usually not that good. Shomron is the largest wine region in Israel.

Samson
Samson is named after the famous Biblical figure, Samson. Besides that, there's nothing special about the wines.

Judean Hills
Judean Hills is tied with the Golan Heights as the best area for wine in Israel. It is an area around the city of Jerusalem, where the nights are cool. It is high in altitude and its wines are the most elegant and refined in Israel. **Cabernet and Shiraz** do well here.

Negev
Negev is desert-like and not much wine is made here.

★ Rome
1) Valle D'Aosta
2) Piemonte
3) Liguria
4) Lombardia
5) Trentino Alto Adige
6) Veneto
7) Friuli
8) Emilia Romagna
9) Toscana
10) Umbria
11) Marche
12) Lazio
13) Abruzzo
14) Molise
15) Campania
16) Puglia
17) Basilicata
18) Calabria
19) Sicilia
20) Sardegna

ITALY

ITALY

Ok, first of all, let me start by saying that there is no way to have a complete book detailing Italian wines without it being tens of thousands of pages. There is so much to talk about, it is absolutely frustrating and sometimes quite discouraging. Clones included, there are over 2,000 different grapes in Italy, most of them with origins native to the land. As overwhelming as that may seem, look at it like this: You now have 2,000 reasons to experience Italian wine.

Before embarking on your journey through Italian wine, you must know that it is the largest producer of wine in the world and most of that wine is never and probably will never be exported. If you don't live in New York, Los Angeles, or any other major city, your contact with the diversity of Italy's wines will be even less. Even with the internet, it's hard to get the wine you want.

Like everything else in Italy, wine is something that is rooted deeply in the land's history. It was made thousands of years ago and the Romans helped spread and plant vineyards across the world. They introduced new techniques and approaches to winemaking. There is now evidence that the Romans were actually the first to invent the type of wine we know now as Champagne.

Over these thousands of years, Italian foods and wines have seemed to form a perfect marriage that is unrivaled anywhere in the world. I believe Italian wine goes best with Italian food, while French wine with French food, and Spanish wine with Spanish food, etc. With Italian food and wine, however, the combination is woven together, almost as if there were Divine intervention. Go to Italy and eat REAL Italian food and you will see what I mean.

Italy is geographically one of the most diverse places on earth. From the Alps to the Mediterranean Sea, its different landscapes offer totally different backgrounds for wines, food, and, obviously, people. The wines, food, people, art, architecture, scenery, etc, are all completely different from region to region, but are somehow harmoniously tied together under one Italian feel.

What you eat and drink in the north of Italy, you probably won't even see in the south. Even the language is spoken differently from region to region. The Italian language is among the ones in the World with the most dialects. It is probably the European language that changed the least since Medieval times.

The history behind Italy shines through every product made there. The wines express the Nobility, Tradition, and Feel of the very region from where they come. With so many grape varieties, it is almost impossible to get bored of Italian wines.

The Regions

Italy has 20 regions, each with their own grapes and different styles of wines. A few regions have the international varieties like Cabernet, Merlot, Chardonnay, and so on. But who cares about those grapes when you have 2,000 new ones to meet and discover? The wines are broken up by region.

All wines and wine regions will not be listed; it would be an unbearably long list to read.

Listed are just a few highlights from the 20 regions of Italy.

NORTH
Piemonte
Liguria
Valle D'Aosta
Lombardia
Emilia-Romagna
Toscana
Friuli-Venezia Giulia
Veneto
Trentino-Alto Adige

CENTRAL
Marche
Lazio
Umbria
Abruzzo
Molise

SOUTH
Campania
Basilicata
Calabria
Puglia

THE ISLANDS
Sicilia
Sardegna

NORTH

PIEMONTE

Whites
Gavi, Arneis, Erbaluce,
Favorita, Timorasso

Reds
Dolcetto, Barbera, Nebbiolo d'Alba
Barolo, Barbaresco, Boca, Gattinara,
Lessona, Bramaterra, Carema, Freisa,
Grignolino, Ruchè,
Pelaverga, Pinerolese Ramìe

Sparkling, Dessert, & Dessert

Moscato D'Asti, Asti Spumante
Brachetto D'Acqui, Barolo Chinato

Whites

Gavi
Made from the **Cortese** grape, this wine boasts very high acidity. It is quite delicate with hints of lime, but it is not quite aromatic. Great with fish and seafood. Not a wine to go crazy for but definitely better with more foods than overpriced oak juice from California.

Arneis
In Piemontese dialect, Arneis means difficult, referring to the difficulty in growing and handling the grape. This wine has beautiful hints of apples, pears, grapefruit, licorice, and nuts. Very versatile and accompanies fish well along with white meats and vegetables. Great with pesto sauces. It is usually from an area called **Roero DOC**; hence, you will see it sometimes as Roero Arneis.

Erbaluce
Erbaluce is a terrific white grape grown mostly in and around the northern town of **Caluso**. It's usually made into dessert wine but, when vinified dry, is a sure crowd pleaser, with its crisp mouth-feel and lively fruit.

Favorita
Favorita is a light bodied wine that is crisp with subtle hints of apple and pear.

Timorasso
Timorasso makes great, structured, full-bodied wines with strong acidity and earthy notes, which is rare for a white wine. It tastes like an aged, white Burgundy. The wine changes from fresh fruit to dried fruit, as it ages, with hints of honey. Very age worthy wines.

Reds

Dolcetto
The name of this grape means "little sweet one". Oddly enough, Dolcetto really isn't sweet. Common flavors of Dolcetto are cherries. The flavors start ripe and fruity in the beginning and end dry, while offering hints of bitter cherry on the finish. Licorice and even coffee can be found. It has low acidity, so it can be drunk young. Dolcetto is the earliest ripening of the 3 main reds of Piemonte. It goes well with pizza and pasta.

Barbera
Barbera is very adaptable and easy to grow, making it one of the most planted grapes in Italy. It is medium bodied with

low tannins and high acidity. Cherry flavors are dominant and, if aged in oak, it will develop tannins, something it is usually low in, and a plummy flavor. This makes a nice pasta wine.

The 3 main Barberas are:

Barbera d'Alba: *Heaviest and most concentrated*

Barbera d'Asti: *Medium*

Barbera del Monferrato: *Lightest and most acidic*

Nebbiolo D'Alba

THE grape of Piemonte. It is very late ripening. Harvest time is usually in November, a time when fog (nebbia) comes and surrounds the vineyards, hence the name Nebbiolo. Same description as Barolo and Barbaresco but Nebbiolo D'Alba is lighter and fruitier than the first two. Great with Bresaola.

Barolo

Made from 100% **Nebbiolo** grapes, this is the king of Italian wines. Tar and roses are the main scents of anything made from Nebbiolo. Full bodied and very complex with high acidity and is tannic as well. Leather, dried herbs, as well as fresh herbs, licorice, and dried cherries, along with many other red fruits. Barolos are very earthy. Austere in their youth, Barolos get better with age. Modern Barolos are made to be drunk earlier. Drink Barolos with heavier, more serious food. Pair the wine with the local food of Piemonte such as beef, lamb, and pasta or risotto with Piemonte's world famous white truffles.

Barbaresco

Made also with **Nebbiolo** and strikingly similar to Barolo. Barbaresco, however, tends to be a little lighter, fruitier, and less tannic, which means it's a little more easy drinking.

Boca

Boca is in the very north of Piemonte and so the **Nebbiolo** grape, here it's called **Spanna**, never fully ripens as quickly as it would further south in Barolo, for example. The wines have higher acidity and so can age longer. They are very elegant.

Gattinara

Gattinara is also further north and its wines, made from **Nebbiolo**, are a little more acidic but can sometimes come close to the powerful Barolos and Barbaresco further south. Additions of the red **Vespolina** to the Nebbiolo is common.

Lessona

Lessona is a very northern and obscure wine area, where only, maybe, two handfuls of producers even make **Nebbiolo** based wine. That being said, the best of Lessona wines are sought after and coveted. Age-worthy and one to store away and save for a special occasion.

Bramaterra
Bramaterra is very similar to Lessona and also located nearby.

Carema
Carema is a northern area of Piemonte and its **Nebbiolo** based wines are lighter and elegant.

Freisa, Grignolino, Ruchè, and Pelaverga
Freisa, Grignolino, Ruchè, and Pelaverga are four grapes I like to call the berry-scented grapes of Piemonte. They all have bright fruit with berry flavors, such as raspberries and strawberries. They are usually light to medium bodied and have good acidity. They are all perfect for appetizers but also stand up to a hefty fondue, called fonduta in Piemonte.

Pinerolese Ramìe
Pinerolese Ramìe is a wine area that makes blend of **Barbera, Bonarda, and Nebbiolo,** but it's most interesting wines come from blends of grapes like **Avanà, Chatus, Bequet, and Avarengo.** Tar, mineral, pine, and cherry fruits are the characteristics of this obscure, yet search worthy, wine.

Sparkling, Dessert, & Dessert

Moscato D'Asti / Asti Spumante
Both wines are very similar and are made with a grape called **Moscato Bianco**. Half way through the fermentation, the wine is put in sealed tanks and the bubbles are trapped. This leaves a good amount of the natural grape sweetness untouched.

Moscato D'Asti is referred to as *frizzante*, while Asti Spumante is just that: *spumante*.

Asti Spumante has more aromatics with higher alcohol and is bubblier.

Moscato D'Asti is fruitier with less alcohol and is less bubbly.

These wines will always have soft and elegant hints of peaches and apricots. Absolutely perfect as an after dinner drink, but just as great for an aperitif. Matches very well with fried foods and shellfish. Though I disagree with pairing sweet wines and dessert together, Moscato D'Asti is one of the very few sweet wines I would pair with a sweet dessert. In fact, enjoying warm slices of Panettone or Pandoro that were toasted in the oven demands a refreshing glass of Moscato D'Asti or Asti Spumante.

Brachetto d'Acqui
Brachetto d'Acqui is a red grape that makes wonderfully aromatic and slightly fizzy wine that is great as an after dinner treat. It also pairs well with the famous chocolate of Piemonte.

Barolo Chinato
Barolo Chinato is a Barolo based wine that is infused with herbs. The word "Chinato" is derived from Cinchona (in Italian China Calisaia) tree bark. Quinine (chinina) in Italian is extracted from the bark and has been historically used medicinally. Quinine and herbs like rhubarb root, star anise, fennel, gentian, citrus peel, juniper, and cardomom seed are infused separately in alcohol and then added to Barolo wine. It is smooth and spicy with flavors of deep, bitter-sweet, orange peel, dried fruits like cherries, figs, and dates, and hints of cloves, and even some eucalyptus. It's like a super luxurious vermouth and happens to go extremely well with another Piemontese specialty : chocolate.

LIGURIA

Whites
Pigato, Vermentino

Reds
Ormeasco, Rossese, Sangiovese

Dessert
Sciacchetrà

Whites

Pigato
A white grape with herbal hints and sharp acidity. It is floral, peachy, and nutty. Very similar to Vermentino, but a little lighter with higher acidity. Great with fish and absolutely perfect with Pesto (this region's pride and joy).

Vermentino
Popular in Liguria, Sardegna, and even coastal Tuscany. In Liguria, it tastes more herbal than usual. As stated above, Vermentino is strikingly similar to Pigato but a little fuller and fruitier. Popular accompaniment to fish.

Reds

Ormeasco
This grape is actually **Dolcetto** under a different name. Very much the same as Dolcetto but a little lighter with earthier hints and more pronounced forest fruits such as red and black berries. Nice with pizza and light pastas. Also good with white meats.

Rossese
From the **Dolceacqua DOC**, it is sometimes known simply as Dolceacqua. Dolceacqua means sweet water. They are light, perfumy, and have moderate acidity. Beaujolais–like in character, it is best served as an accompaniment to light fare.

Sangiovese
One of the most planted grapes in Italy, possibly THE most planted, it makes its appearance in Liguria as an earthier version of the Tuscan Sangiovese based wines. More earthy hints of mushrooms are prevalent. Great with pasta and beans.

Dessert

Sciacchetrà
The famed dessert wine of this area is nearly impossible to get. Very limited quantities are ever made. Using **Bosco, Albarola, and Vermentino** grapes, Sciacchetrà dessert wines are one of those rare sweet treats that come once every third blue moon.

VALLE D'AOSTA

Whites
Petit Arvine
Blanc de Morgex et de La Salle

Reds
Nebbiolo, Petit Rouge, Fumin

Whites

Petite Arvine
White grape with high acidity. Petit Arvine makes crisp wines with citrus and apple hints. Also made as sweet or semi-sweet wine. Hard to find.

Blanc de Morgex et de La Salle
Blanc de Morgex et de La Salle is made with the high acidity white grape called **Prié Blanc** that has herbaceous tones with hints of hay. It's a wonderful white that pairs well with many foods.

Reds

Nebbiolo
Here, the Piemontese grape is called **Picotendro** and is lighter and fruitier with a higher level of acidity than most Nebbiolos in Piedmont, given its much more Northern climate.

Petit Rouge
Petit Rouge is a very popular grape in the region and produces wines that are tangy and berry hinted.

Fumin
Fumin is a red grape that is generally blended but has been slowly, but surely, being made into wine as a mono-varietal. Syrah-like, with herbaceous and tobacco characteristics, plump fruit and soft tannins.

LOMBARDIA

Whites
Riesling

Sparkling
Franciacorta

Reds
Valtellina, Oltrepò Pavese
Sangue di Giuda

Whites

Riesling
The best white grape makes an appearance in northern Italy but, in the Oltrepò Pavese area, it can produce one of the top whites in Italy. The high altitude and mountain cool climate help produce a lighter style Riesling that finishes crisp and dry like Rieslings from the nearby Friuli region.

Sparkling

Franciacorta
A DOC in the north. One can call this Italy's response to Champagne, but, in reality, Champagne is France's answer to Italian sparkling wine. It is now known that the Romans enjoyed sparkling wines way back then. Although typically French grapes (**Chardonnay, Pinot Noir, Pinot Meunier**) are used, the quality of good Franciacorta comes at usually half the price of the French sparkling wines.

Reds

Valtellina
The best **Nebbiolo** in Lombardia comes from this area. It is locally called **Chiavennasca**. Nebbiolo here is at its lightest and most elegant.
There are 4 Delimited Vineyards (A.K.A. Grand Crus of Valtellina) : **Sassella, Grumello, Inferno, and Valgella**. There is also an appassimento of Nebbiolo, meaning it's like an Amarone but made from Nebbiolo and in the region of Lombardia. You may see **Sfursat or Sforzato** on the label for the appassimento wines, meaning the grapes are dried first before pressing.

Oltrepò Pavese
The name breaks down like this: Oltrepò (over the Pò river) and Pavese (in the province of Pavia). This area produces very good **Pinot Noir**. Its cool climate is perfect for this delicate and hard to handle grape.

Sangue di Giuda
Sangue di Giuda is a slightly fizzy and slightly sweet, red wine made from **Barbera, Croatina, and Uva Rara**. It's also from Oltrepò Pavese. It's a fun party wine or a nice dessert alternative.

EMILIA-ROMAGNA

Whites
Albana, Famoso

Reds
Lambrusco, Gutturnio
Sangiovese di Romagna
Centesimino

Sparkling
Ortrugo, Pignoletto

Whites

Albana
Albana is usually nothing special, unless made by serious producers. In those cases, Albana can reach new heights, especially if made into "orange wines".

Famoso
Famoso means famous in Italian, which is funny because this grape by the same name was never famous but, starting in the second decade of the 2000's, has been attaining fame. It's a great white grape capable of making floral wines with aromas and flavors of peach, apricot, orange, banana, and apple. Amazing white. Great for a party starter or with small plates.

Reds

Lambrusco
Often incorrectly viewed as commercial, sweet wine, Lambrusco is a red grape that is capable of making incredible wines, whether **dry (secco), slightly sweet (amabile), or sweet (dolce)**. At its best when produced in **Sorbara**, where the sandy soils make it refined and elegant. In **Castelvetro**, the Lambrusco variety called **Grasparossa** makes wines that are

darker, a bit more robust, and tannic. Lambrusco is slightly effervescent and can be sweet, semisweet, or dry. They are meant to be drunk young. A fun **rosé version** is also made. If you drink Lambrusco and it reminds you of the real, artisanal, balsamic vinegar of Emilia Romagna, called **Aceto Balsamico Tradizionale**, it's because Lambrusco is one of the grapes used to make the World's most prized vinegars. Great with chestnuts and rosy hams. Also great with any of the famous, cured meats of the region, like Prosciutto, Culatello, Mortadella, and Salame, and cheeses, especially Parmigiano Reggiano.

Gutturnio

A blend of **Barbera and Bonarda** that may be vinified dry, sweet, or even into a frizzante. Cherries and chocolate are typical notes. Gutturnio comes from the Latin Gutturnium, meaning imbibing cup and refers to the white, ceramic bowl style cups the wine was historically served in and continues to be enjoyed in the exact same way, even today. This is a great wine to go with what the region is famous for : Lasagne Verdi.

N.B. Bonarda makes wine that is plummy and cherry hinted, with a slightly bitter finish. There are many kinds of Bonarda from Piemonte, Lombardia, Emilia Romagna, and Argentina. There is great confusion and I am here to clear it up. The Bonarda from Piemonte (A.K.A. Bonarda Piemontese) is the REAL Bonarda (Bonarda proper) and hard to find. It is blended with Nebbiolo and Croatina to make Gattinara. In Lombardia, Bonarda is called Uva Rara except in Oltrepò Pavese, where the Croatina grape is strangely called Bonarda di Gattinara or Bonarda di Cavaglia. In Emilia Romagna, Bonarda is also called Uva Rara, except in Colli Piacentini where the Croatina grape is also strangely called Bonarda di Gattinara or Bonarda di Cavaglia. *The most important* one is the Croatina from Oltrepò Pavese and Colli Piacentini. Then, in Argentina, Bonarda is probably neither of the top 3, and may be California's Charbono, which may be related to Dolcetto.

Sangiovese di Romagna

The Sangiovese wines here have less acidity and tannins than those from nearby Chianti. Still displays the typical red fruits like raspberries and cherries.

Centesimino

Centesimino is often used for dessert wine production but makes an interesting, citrus flavored red, when vinified dry.

Sparkling

Ortrugo

Usually made into frizzante and often blended with Malvasia. Crisp with notes of apples.

Pignoletto

Another white grape usually made into frizzante, with flavors of lime, citrus, and green apple. Very crisp.

TOSCANA

Whites
Vernaccia, Vermentino

Reds
Chianti, Brunello di Montalcino
Rosso di Montalcino
Vino Nobile di Montepulciano
Carmignano, Morellino di Scansano
Super Tuscan, Bolgheri, Pugnitello

Dessert
Vin Santo

Whites

Vernaccia di San Gimignano
The very first to receive DOC status in Italy, this famed wine comes from the even more famous town of San Gimignano. High acidity and nice citrus notes. Nice with shrimp and Tuscan beans.

Vermentino
Vermentino is mostly grown on the island of Sardegna, facing Tuscany, but it does well on the mainland, too. It does well in Liguria as well, but Tuscany and Sardegna are the best. Amazing fish wine. Also great with vegetables.

Reds

Chianti
Everyone knows this one. Ranging from mediocre to excellent, Chianti is made always with a dominant percentage of **Sangiovese**. Blended in are other grapes like **Canaiolo, Colorino, Trebbiano, and Malvasia**. Very dry and boasts very high acidity, Chianti is popular for its cherry and raspberry characteristics. It typically can offer hints of tea on the finish. **Chianti Classico** wines, coming from a sub-region called Classico, are considered the best. Classico bottles are easily identified by their **Black Rooster logo**, in Italian called **Gallo Nero**. Outside of Classico is **Rùfina**, whose wines are believed to be among the best as well. **Chianti Riserva** wines are aged longer and prized more than regular Chiantis. Outside of the Classico area, wines that meet more strict requirements can be labeled **Superiore**. All good Chianti are stunning matches with pasta and tomato sauce.

Brunello di Montalcino
Incredible. Brunello is a larger version of the **Sangiovese** grape. It actually harvests quite early, so it usually avoids October rains. Very big, full bodied with high acidity and a lot of tannins. Can age very long thanks to its well balanced structure. Essentially, a bigger, better, and more refined version of Chianti. This is a serious wine, perfect for hearty meals and special occasions.

Rosso di Montalcino
This is basically a **junior Brunello**. It is not aged as long. It is fruitier, slightly lighter, and usually half the price. Rosso di Montalcino is a steal.

Vino Nobile di Montepulciano
The name means noble wine. Remember, this wine is from Tuscany, a place that, throughout time, has best exemplified nobility. Good Vino Nobile is pure class and elegance. Made from **Prugnolo**, another larger version of the **Sangiovese grape**, this is a wine for pastas, light meats, and bean dishes. **N.B.** Do not confuse with Montepulciano D'Abruzzo, a wine made from Montepulciano grapes in a region called Abruzzo.

Carmignano

Carmignano was the first Super Tuscan type of wine about 100 years before winemakers were even promoting their wines as Super Tuscans. In fact, it was the first DOC to be legally allowed to blend Cabernet into its wines and keep the DOC designation. It eventually became a DOCG. The wines, made mostly from **Sangiovese**, benefit from the addition of the hefty **Cabernet Sauvignon**.

Morellino di Scansano

Morellino is another clone of **Sangiovese** and from Scansano, where its sandy soils, much further south in Tuscany, give the wine a soft and plump mouth-feel. Great with meats and bean dishes.

Super Tuscan

These are wines made by either **unapproved grapes** (Cabernet, Merlot etc), **unapproved winemaking methods** (smaller, non-traditional oak barrels), or an **unapproved composition** (using 100% Sangiovese). Since these wines break the rules, they may only be labeled Vino da Tavola (Table Wine). This should not imply that they are inferior, when, in fact, some Super Tuscans can actually be better than DOCG wines from Tuscany. Super Tuscans can be either red or white; however, the reds being more popular and usually better wine.

Bolgheri

Bolgheri is a fairly new DOC located in a coastal area called **Maremma** that encompasses the southern portion of Tuscany and the northern portion of Lazio. Its wines are usually Bordeaux blends, with **Cabernet and Merlot** quite prominent; of course, **Sangiovese** also makes an appearance. These wines are serious heavy hitters and are usually reserved for special occasions. Great with a nice Bistecca alla Fiorentina, a gigantic, beef Porterhouse cut for 2 or more people.

Pugnitello

Pugnitello is a rare grape that was saved from almost extinction. Its wines are dark with blackberry fruits, has good structure, and is good for ageing, given it has good acidity and tannins. Can also be blended with **Foglia Tonda**.

Dessert

Vin Santo

In Tuscany, Vin Santo is typically made with the white grapes Trebbiano, Malvasia, and Canaiolo. In **Pomino DOC**, Tuscany, they actually make a red Vin Santo using **Sangiovese, Cabernet, Merlot, and Cabernet Franc**. To make Vin Santo, the grapes are first dried hanging in bunches. The grapes are then put into *caratelli* (small barrels) with the *madre*. Madre is the wine left over from the previous year, which itself, of course, contains a little from the previous year and so on, etc. The wine goes through an oxidation process, which gives Vin Santo its typical nutty flavor. Some Vin Santo wines are sweet and, therefore, best suited for dessert, while others may be dry and better used as an aperitif. Great with biscotti.

FRIULI-VENEZIA GIULIA

Whites
Pinot Grigio, Tocai Friulano
Riesling, Ribolla Gialla
Vitovska, Malvasia

Reds
Refesco, Pignolo
Schiopettino (Ribolla Nera)
Tazzelenghe, Terrano
Cabernet, Cabernet Franc, Merlot

Dessert
Picolit, Verduzzo

Whites

Pinot Grigio
The most popular Italian white in the U.S.. Pinot Grigio in northern Italy is dry, crisp, and light bodied. Nutty and spicy, it is great as an aperitif and with appetizers.

Tocai Friulano
The world Tocai appears in many different countries with slight differences in spelling and complete differences in the identity of the grapes. Tocai Friualano from Friuli is fleshy and minerally, with high acidity. Hints of nutmeg and almonds, as well as peach and pear are common. Excellent wine to go with Baccalà (codfish), as well as almost any other fish.

N.B. Sadly, in 2007, it became illegal to label wine bottles made from this grape Tocai Friulano due to a European Union ruling that lamented it led people to assume it was Tokaji from Hungary, a wine made from a blend of grapes, none of which are Tocai Friulano. The most famous type of Hungarian Tokaji is the Tokaji Aszú, a sweet, dessert wine. Given the Italian wine is a dry white made from Tocai Friulano grapes, the Hungarian Tokaji has no Italian Tocai Friulano in it, Tokaji is mostly known for its dessert version, Aszu, and 99% of people have (sadly) never heard of Tokaji until this ruling, I refuse to call Tocai Friulano simply "Friulano" as the winemakers are dictated to sell it. I love the Hungarian one but I also love common sense; it's not illegal......yet.

Riesling
You should know that I am a staunch advocate for Riesling. The best is, of course, from Germany, but Friuli turns out some pretty good ones. The Rieslings in Friuli are drier and crisper than German ones. Goes well with almost anything.

Ribolla Gialla
One of my favorites when made well. Hints of apple and lemon, subtle with excellent balance and high acidity. One of the best seafood wines, period. Age-worthy.

Vitovska
Vitovska is an extremely minerally and chalky, rare white treat from Friuli that is an either love it or hate it type of wine. Most wine lovers, the very few who have heard of it, love it. Very age-worthy.

Malvasia
Malvasia is usually made into dessert wines but, when vinifed dry, is an elegant, yet explosively flavored, wine that pairs well with any type of seafood and fried foods.

Reds

Refosco
This Friuli red exhibits grassy characteristics with a bitter dry finish. Deep colored and dense. Dark chocolate and plums are also typical. When made correctly, it can be very good.

Pignolo
Sometimes compared to Brunello, Pignolo wines are dense and dark. High tannins with bitter cherry, black fruits like blackberries, and slightly spicy. Good match with Pasta.

Schioppettino
Also called **Ribolla Nera** (the black version of Ribolla Gialla), Schioppettino has Syrah characteristics and, therefore, is quite Rhône like. It is difficult to grow and very hard to ripen. If made well, it can be spicy and peppery, with blackberry and raspberry hints, and high acidity. Nice with roasted meats.

Tazzelenghe
In Friulian dialect, Tazzelenghe means "tongue cutter". Obviously, as the name implies, this red is highly acidic. Dark and deep, good Tazzelenghe is not easy to get in the States.

Terrano
Terrano may actually be a clone of Refosco and tastes like it were a cross between Refosco and Aglianico. It's dark and mysterious and goes well with hearty meals.

Cabernet, Merlot, and Cabernet Franc
These three international grape varieties are quite popular here, but they are made very differently than elsewhere. Here, they are not as full bodied and have less fruit than California ones. Herbal hints, tobacco, and bell pepper are more common due to the cooler climate of Friuli.

Dessert

Picolit
A floral, white grape that can be dry or sweet; the latter being the best. It has a honeyed nectar hint. It is usually blended with dry whites to add sweetness and character.

Verduzzo
May be bone dry or sweet. Better known for its sweet version, the Verduzzo grape has high acidity and lemony hints.

VENETO

Whites :
Bianco di Custoza , Soave, Lugana
Incrocio Manzoni, Vespaiola

Reds :
Bardolino, Valpolicella,
Amarone, Ripasso

Sparkling :
Prosecco, Lessini Durello

Dessert :
Recioto di Soave, Recioto di Gambellara
Recioto della Valpolicella, Vespaiola

After Dinner :
Grappa

Whites

Bianco di Custoza
Usually a blend of either **Garganega, Riesling, Tocai, Trebbiano, and Malvasia**. Getting better every year, Bianco di Custoza makes its mark in the wine world. Typically offers soft hints of peach and lighter in body than other Veneto whites. Perfect as an aperitif or with snacks. Great with light fish.

Soave
Made from **Garganega and Trebbiano** grapes. Typically light to medium bodied. Citrus notes and nutty hints are common. More producers are making better Soave now than ever. Try it with light fish.

Lugana
Lugana is a wine region near the beautiful lake, Lago di Garda, and is shared between Lombardia and Veneto. It's mostly known for its white wine made from **Trebbiano di Lugana**, which may be related to Verdicchio. It's a lively wine and easy to like. Great with seafood and even the veal-tuna mix, Vitello Tonnato.

Incrocio Manzoni
Incrocio Manzoni is a cross between **Riesling and Pinot Bianco** and makes a lively, zesty, clean, food friendly white.

Vespaiola
Vespaiola is a terrific white grape usually used to make dessert wine but, when vinified dry, exhibits all the wonderful, aromatic fruity notes that make it loved but with a dry finish. I love dry wines made from grapes that are usually meant for dessert wines but instead enjoyed with food; they are more lively and interesting.

Reds

Bardolino
From **Corvina, Rondinella, Molinara, and Negrara**, it's similar to Valpolicella but not quite as good. Bardolino is usually lighter bodied. Also made in a Rosato (Rosé) version called **Chiaretto**.

Valpolicella
In the region's dialect, Valpolicella means "valley of the many cellars". **Corvina, Molinara and Rondinella** are used. **Valpolicella Classico** are the best ones. Done right, it's a favorite. Hints of cherry and almonds, with high acidity, Valpolicellas are dry. Great with pasta and tomato sauce, rabbit, squash, etc.

Amarone
This is one of the most amazing things in life, period! Amarone literally means "big bitter". The full name is actually **Recioto della Valpolicella Amarone**. Recioto comes from the dialect word "recie", meaning ears. Traditionally, the side clusters of the grape bunches were picked. It was believed that they received the most sunlight and therefore were better. **Corvina, Molinara, and Rondinella** grapes are air dried on trays in ventilated rooms, sometimes up to four months. The grapes lose about half their water content and shrivel up. The sugars and flavors become ultra intensified. Essentially, the wine is made by pressing semi-raisins instead of just grapes. This process is called appassimento. When the wine ferments, the producer has two options. If he/she *does not* let it ferment all the way to complete dryness, then it is essentially a sweet dessert wine. This is labeled **Recioto della Valpolicella**. If the wine is fully fermented all the way to complete dryness, then it is called **Recioto della Valpolicella Amarone** or just simply **AMARONE**. Even though it is vinified dry, it never really seems so. The first swirl and sniff might indicate that the wine is very fruity, maybe even sweet. Once you taste, you get a fruity sweetness that turns bitter sweet. Then arrives the explosion of taste. Bitter chocolate, cherries, bitter cherries, plums, almonds, and much more. The great thing about good Amarone is that it offers so much but somehow manages to put it all together harmoniously in a perfectly balanced package. In winemaking, balance is hard to achieve and Amarone makes that task even harder. Due to the lengthy and expensive process used in making it, the customer will pay a healthy amount for good Amarone. When buying Amarone, avoid the new style ones that are so exaggerated, they really give Amarone a bad name. Please do yourself a favor and set aside a special occasion to drink traditional Amarone.

Ripasso
The word ripasso means to repass. It refers to the Valpolicella wine that is repassed through the Amarone skins and pulp from the prior batch. It picks up body and flavor. In short, Ripasso is like a junior Amarone or like a cross between Valpolicella and Amarone. It also comes at a much smaller price than Amarone. Ripasso is a steal.

Sparkling

Prosecco
This grape is used for producing one of Italy's most famous sparklers. Prosecco is the wine used in making the very popular Bellini cocktail. Bellini is a drink that consists of Prosecco and peach nectar, made famous at Harry's Bar in Venice. Prosecco is dry with hints of almond and citrus. Good Prosecco is well worth a try and, in some cases, much better than some $40 bottles of Champagne. In the early 2000's, the name Prosecco officially became the area where it is produced and the grape, once also called Prosecco, was to be changed to the original name, **Glera**. Either way you call it, most Prosecco is made with the **Charmat-Martinotti** method.

Lessini Durello
Made from a grape called **Durella**, which is confusing, given it ends with the letter "a" but the wine region is spelled with an "o" at the end. Makes great sparkling wine with apple and citrus hints. Has good structure.

Dessert

Recioto di Soave
Made from **Garganega and Trebbiano** grapes, Recioto di Soave is made using the passito grapes from the appassimento process. These wines are honeyed and peachy, with apricot and almond hints, and just plain delicious.

Recioto di Gambellara
Very similar to the Recioto di Soave. This one however is even harder to find in the States.

Recioto della Valpolicella
As described earlier in the Amarone section, this wine is made by stopping the fermentation earlier before it completely reaches dry. It is the step prior to actual Amarone. It is Port-like and considered a dessert wine. If the fermentation is carried out fully, then it is dry and considered Amarone.

Vespaiola
This white grape has a very high sugar content. It produces one of my favorite dessert wines. When the grapes are dried, it can be blended with Tocai and Garganega to produce a luscious dessert wine that is rich and velvety. Soft hints of apricots, baked pears, honey, brown spice, hazelnut, and even vanilla. The high sugar content is remarkably balanced by the grape's natural high level of acidity. Absolutely a must try. Some of the best dessert Vespaiolas come from the **Breganze Torcolato DOC**.

After Dinner

Grappa
There are many after dinner drinks in the world and Italy has more than plenty. Some of the famous ones are: Limoncello, Amaro, and Grappa. I only will discuss Grappa, given it is made from grapes. This is meant to be a wine book, so whatever is linked to wine will be mentioned. Grappa is made from grape pomace. Pomace is the left over pulp, skins, seeds, and stems, which remain after the juice has been pressed out. Initially, Grappa was considered a by-product. Eventually, wineries made their own Grappa to make a little extra money. Winery Grappas are never anything special and are made to help pay the bills. There are however whole companies dedicated solely to the production of Grappa. They do not make wine or anything else. JUST GRAPPA. These are the ones whose products you should seek out and try. Veneto is the ultimate place for Grappa, although it is made all over Italy. The city, **Bassano del Grappa**, located in the Veneto is Heaven for this after dinner drink. There are also Grappas infused with fruits, herbs, and even chamomile. It may take some getting used to, but Grappa (like many Italian aperitifs and after dinner drinks) is meant to aid in digestion. Grappa is best served cool to cold.

TRENTINO-ALTO ADIGE

Whites:
Pinot Grigio, Pinot Bianco, Moscato Giallo, Nosiola, Sylvaner, Kerner, Traminer

Reds:
Lagrein, Teroldego
Marzemino, Schiava
Enantio

Dessert:
Vin Santo
Moscato Rosa

Whites

Pinot Grigio
Trentino, a region noted world wide for its apples, also turns out some great Pinot Grigio. The soils and climate are perfect for this grape to prosper. Typical tastes such as nuttiness and spice are present.

Pinot Bianco
Pinot Biancos are medium to full bodied, crisp, and yet creamy. Full flavored and lively with floral notes and fruit hints of apple and pear. Different styles of this grape exist and it's hard not to love each one.

Moscato Giallo
Moscato Giallo is one of the many sub-varieties of the Moscato grape and is usually made into dessert wines but, when vinifed dry, is a flavor bomb that livens the palate with its peachy and apricot aromas and flavors.

Nosiola
Nosiola is also a grape generally destined for dessert wine production but can make beautiful, elegant, dry whites that are great for sipping or for appetizers.

Sylvaner
Sylvaner is mostly found in Germany and Alsace, France but is also at home here. It is crisp and light with earthy and floral hints.

Kerner
Kerner is a white grape that's actually a **cross** of the **white Riesling** and the **red grape Schiava**. It's one of my favorite go-to's and everyone loves it for its refreshing and lively, aromatic fruit. Its crisp acidity allows it to pair well with almost any food.

Traminer
The main grape of which there are many sub-varieties. Very aromatic and honeyed.

Reds

Lagrein
Thought to originate from the river by the same name. There are two kinds: **Lagrein Dunkel and Lagrein Kretzer** (Rosato / Rosé). The Lagrein Dunkel is dark, with grassy hints and chocolate and plum characteristics. Lagrein is a grape with pretty good acidity and a low level of mild tannins. Lagrein Kretzer is the Rosato (rosé) version.

Teroldego
Mostly produced in the Rotaliano plain. Teroldego is a grape that makes medium bodied wines with grassiness, licorice, and plum notes. Nice with hams and pasta with cream sauces.

Marzemino
This grape is thought to be related to Teroldego. Very similar characteristics. There is also a grape called **Rebo**, which is a cross between Marzemino and Merlot.

Schiava
This grape's name is derived from the Italian word for slave. What is the meaning? Who knows?!? Schiava is barely red, with hints of strawberry and even bacon. A light wine perfect for appetizers.

Enantio
Enantio is a rare grape also called Lambrusco a Foglia Frastagliata, which is not related to Lambrusco from Emilia Romagna, but can be also found sparkling, like Lambrusco, and still, as well. Dark colored with high acidity. Spicy and likes to be aged in oak. Flavors of black pepper, licorice, tobacco, and clove.

Dessert

Vin Santo
Here, in Trentino, Vin Santo is made with the **Nosiola** grape. Not as good as Tuscan or Umbrian Vin Santo, but it is good with its crisp acidity and lightness. It is very hard to find this Trentino Vin Santo.

Moscato Rosa
Makes great dry wines but it's famous for the aromatic and pink colored dessert wines.

CENTRAL

MARCHE

Whites :
Verdicchio, Passerina

Reds :
Rosso Conero, Rosso Piceno
Vernaccia Nera
Lacrima di Morro D'Alba

Whites

Verdicchio
The name of this grape derives from the Italian word for green, which is *verde*. It is verde because the grapes remain very green in color, even when fully ripe. This grape makes wine with a resiny feel and pineapple hint. It also exhibits green herbs, anise, Bosc pears, and green apples. This highly acidic grape is best known when producing wines in and around the city of Jesi. Look for **Verdicchio dei Castelli di Jesi** for the better ones but the **Verdicchio di Matelica** can also be great. They are also quite age-worthy. Great with shellfish and obviously pasta with shellfish.

Passerina
Passerina makes fun white wine with citrus and melon notes and peachy aromatics. Great wine for shellfish.

Reds

Rosso Conero
Considered to be Marche's best red. Made from at least 85% **Montepulciano** and a maximum of 15% **Sangiovese**. These wines have high acidity and deep cherry fruit. Great with chicken dishes and, of course, pasta of many kinds.

Rosso Piceno
Usually **half Montepulciano / half Sangiovese**. This wine comes off as a softer and fruitier Chianti. Can be a good, simple value.

Vernaccia Nera
Vernaccia Nera is a very unique wine from the **Serrapetrona** area of Le Marche and has some heavy, peppery notes and dark fruit that give it a mysterious personality. Great with hearty fare.

Lacrima di Morro D'Alba
Lacrima di Morro D'Alba makes wines that are soft and plump and similar to Beaujolais.

LAZIO

Whites :
Frascati

Reds
Cesanese, Aleatico, Grechetto Rosso
Cabernet, Merlot, Shiraz

Whites

Frascati
A DOC zone that uses **Malvasia, Trebbiano, and Greco**. Very light, dry, and crisp. Should be drunk carefree, as it is wine of little importance. Essentially, a thirst quencher.

Reds

Cesanese
Cesanese is one of the few, local, red grapes of Lazio, which isn't usually that great; Lazio is white wine country. The ones that are good have hints of plum and cranberry and are good pairing options with Cacio e Pepe and even a nice Porchetta, roast pork.

Aleatico
Aleatico usually makes dessert wines but, when vinified dry, is aromatic and pleasant to drink.

Grechetto Rosso
A rare grape that is usually used in blends. It has been finding its way into the bottle as a mono-varietal with impressive results. It's dark and fragrant and very interesting. Definitely a wine for meats and hearty pastas.

Cabernet / Merlot / Shiraz
The soils here are perfect for international varieties such as these three. Lazio does better with these than their own indigenous grapes. On the southern coast of Lazio, the soils are great for Syrah, which can tolerate heat and does not overproduce even in these fertile soils.

UMBRIA

Whites :
Orvieto
Grechetto Bianco

Reds :
Sagrantino di Montefalco
Montefalco Rosso

Dessert :
Passito di Sagrantino

Whites

Orvieto
A DOC zone that produces wine made from **Trebbiano, Malvasia, Grechetto, and Verdello**. Similar to Lazio's Frascati, but much better. Great as an aperitif wine and also with appetizers and light meats such as chicken.

Grechetto Bianco
Usually blended to make Orvieto, producers in Umbria are finding its peachy notes are great enough to be made on its own. Crisp and refreshing.

Reds

Sagrantino di Montefalco
From the DOC zone of Montefalco, this wine is made with the Sagrantino grape. Very deep in color and very tannic. It is believed to be the most tannic grape in Italy and maybe the world. Too much tannin can be rough on the palate, but Sagrantino's tannins are surprisingly sweet in proportion to its high amount and quiet supple and soft. It offers smokiness with bitter cherry hints. Great with pasta and Umbria's famous black truffles. Terrific partner with truffle cheese. Also great with an array of pork products and dishes.

Montefalco Rosso
A wine made with **Sagrantino and Sangiovese**. Not as powerful as straight Sagrantino but well worth the try. This wine can also be made using the appassimento process.

Dessert

Passito di Sagrantino
Passito di Sagrantino is a red dessert wine made from the dried grapes of **Sagrantino**. This passito is voluptuous and rich and a perfect way to finish any hearty meal, especially one including meat and/or Umbria's famous black truffles.

ABRUZZO

Whites :
Trebbiano d'Abruzzo
Pecorino, Coccociola

Rosato :
Cerasuolo d'Abruzzo

Reds :
Montepulciano d'Abruzzo

Whites

Trebbiano d' Abruzzo
A white grape that produces high yields. Very simple, dry, and crisp. Nothing special, unless made by artisanal producers who can transform the wines from this grape into wine gems.

Pecorino
Pecorino in Italian means sheep's milk cheese; pecora is sheep. The reason the white grape is called Pecorino is because the sheep of the area used to love to eat the grapes while grazing and wandering the vineyards. It makes interesting wines that are crisp and floral.

Cococciola
Cococciola is a personal favorite. It tastes like dry Riesling and is extremely versatile.

Rosato

Cerasuolo d'Abruzzo
Cerasuolo d'Abruzzo is a rosato (rosé) wine and its name means cherry red, given the wine is a medium to dark cherry red color that has full-flavored notes of cherries and strawberries, too. Not to be confused with Cerasuolo di Vittoria, a Sicilian red wine.

Reds

Montepulciano d' Abruzzo
The grape is Montepulciano. This is not to be confused with Vino Nobile di Montepulciano, which is a Tuscan wine from the town named Montepulciano. In Abruzzo, the Montepulciano grape is very popular. Typically, Montepulciano is fruity and quite simple. It is generally added in blends to add fruit and spiciness. A perfect wine for Bucatini all'Amatriciana.

MOLISE

Reds
Montepulciano

Montepulciano
Molise is a small region that borrows a lot of its wine culture from neighboring regions. The Montepulciano grape seems to work best for this region. The style of the wine is strikingly similar to that made in Abruzzo. At one point, these two regions were collectively known as Abruzzi e Molise.

SOUTH

CAMPANIA

Whites :
Greco di Tufo, Fiano di Avellino
Falanghina, Campi Flegrei
Coda di Volpe, Ischia
Ravello, Pallagrello Bianco
Lacryma Christi del Vesuvio Bianco

Reds :
Aglianico, Taurasi,
Falerno del Massico,
Lacryma Christi del Vesuvio Rosso
Casavecchia, Pallagrello Rosso
Cilento, Gragnano

Sparkling :
Asprinio

Whites

Greco di Tufo

Greco is a white grape grown all over the south of Italy but is most comfortable in Campania, specifically in and around a small town named Tufo. If made correctly, Greco di Tufo can be stunning. Nutty, slightly smoky, with soft hints of fruit. This wine graciously boasts high acidity. Perfect with almost any kind of fish and shellfish. Great with light white meats. Perfect for appetizers.

Fiano di Avellino

Fiano is a white grape that is aromatic, flowery, spicy, and slightly honeyed. Its nuttiness is complimented by its typical peach characteristics. Very good with fish. Highly regarded to be Campania's best white; I believe it is second to good Greco di Tufo. Very age-worthy.

Falanghina

Considered to be in between Greco and Fiano, taste wise. It has high acidity like Greco and a fruit profile similar to that of Fiano. Very much loved worldwide and versatile. Great with any dish that calls for white wine.

Campi Flegrei

Campi Flegrei is a super volcano that has its caldera mostly under water. It is known for its gaseous activity and bubbling, heated water from the ground. Scary, but the wines are not. Though some red wine from **Piedirosso** is made, the area is mostly known for its whites, made usually from **Falanghina**, and are known for their minerality.

Coda di Volpe

Coda di Volpe means tail of the fox in Italian and it gets its name from the fact that the grape clusters look like a fox's tail. It is usually blended with other grapes but on its own is known for medium bodied wines that are citrusy and flavorful. Great with seafood.

Ischia

Ischia white wine is lovely and crisp and made from local grapes like **San Lunardo, Forastera, and Biancolella**. Ideal for seafood and even rabbit.

Ravello

Ravello is one of the most beautiful towns in the World, perched atop the middle of the Amalfi Coast. It's the best wine producing area of the sunny and stunning Coast. Furore and Tramonti also make great stuff but Ravello is the king of the

Costa d'Amalfi DOC. The town makes serious whites, usually from blends of **Coda di Volpe, Falangina, San Nicola, and Greco**.

Pallagrello Bianco
This is a star grape that makes wines that have honeyed notes of melon, grapefruit, with a nutty background. This wine is as serious as many revered, classic, French Burgundies but at only half the price.

Lacryma Christi del Vesuvio Bianco
The name means "Tears Of Christ". A wine area from the slopes of Mt. Vesuvius that are usually blends of **Coda di Volpe, Verdeca, Falanghina, Greco, and Fiano.**

Reds

Aglianico
Aglianico is the most popular red grape of Campania. It makes powerful wines that are deep, dark, and funky. It's not mild in any way and its lovers prefer it that way. Great wine for truffles, meats, and hearty pastas.

Taurasi
Made primarily from the **Aglianico** grape, Taurasi is the purest and best expression of this grape. It can be blended with little amounts of Piedirosso, Sangiovese, and Barbera. Full bodied, high acidity, with dark berry fruits and a smoky feel. It is nicknamed "The Barolo of the South". Very austere in its youth, Taurasi gets better with age. Perfect for lamb or heavy pasta dishes.

Falerno del Massico
Falerno del Massico is mostly known for its **Aglianico**, which is hefty and age worthy, with dark fruit flavors.

Lacryma Christi del Vesuvio Rosso
The name means "Tears Of Christ" and its red blends from Mt. Vesuvius' slopes are made with **Piedirosso, Sciascinoso (Olivella Nera), and Aglianico**.

Casavecchia
An ancient grape that's reappearing. It's a dark wine usually used for blending with Pallagerello Rosso but on its own is age worthy, with soft tannins, herbaceous, and flavors of leather and black fruits.

Pallagrello Rosso
A peppery and spicy red usually blended with Casavecchia for age worthy wines.

Cilento
Cilento wines are like the people from that area : gentle, elegant, and fun. Its **Aglianicos** are among the fruitiest in Campania and blended with Piedirosso.

Gragnano
Gragnano is a town known for producing some of the best pasta in the World. They also are known for their famous "pizza wine" by the same name, Gragnano. It's a slightly, fizzy red, that is similar to a dry, but fruity, Lambrusco. Perfect with pizza, panuozzo (a pizza sandwich), and cheese and cured meats. In Vino Veritas was and still is proud to have been one of the very first and few to sell Gragnano anywhere in the World, outside of Gragnano. Mostly from **Piedirosso** and maybe some **Aglianico**. The nearby Lettere makes similar wine, named **Lettere**. Chilled, both are party favorites.

Sparkling

Asprinio is highly acidic, so it makes great, sparkling wines in the Aversa part of Campania.

BASILICATA

Aglianico del Vulture
Hailing from Vulture (an extinct volcano), this Aglianico based wine is similar to that of Taurasi. Its structure is even bolder and it is more austere than Taurasi. Aglianico del Vulture also benefits from long ageing.

CALABRIA

Whites : Cirò Bianco

Reds : Cirò Rosso, Magliocco, Savuto, Scavigna, Lamezia Terme

Rosato : Cirò Rosato

Dessert : Montonico, Greco di Bianco

Whites

Cirò Bianco
Made from **Greco Bianco**, a clone of Greco di Tufo from Campania. It is medium bodied, full flavored, with citrusy and peachy notes and with good acidity. A terrific seafood wine. Greco Di Bianco is also from Calabria but is a dessert wine and probably not related.

Reds

Cirò Rosso
A very unique and pleasantly unusual wine made from an obscure grape called **Gaglioppo** which is light colored, with hints of dried citrus, figs, and bitter chocolate. High alcohol and high acidity. Great with Calabria's famous salumi.

Magliocco
Magliocco comes in two varieties : the dark, tannic, and plump **Magliocco Dolce** from Northern Calabria and the **Magliocco Canino** from further South, which is more like Gaglioppo, with its bright, red fruit and spiciness.

Savuto / Scavigna / Lamezia Terme
These 3 DOC's are so close, they're almost one atop the other and they make great reds from **Gaglioppo, Greco Nero, Nerello Mascalese, Nerello Cappuccio, and Magliocco**, among others.

Rosato

Cirò Rosato
A full bodied, spicy, cherry and strawberry flavored show-stopper from **Gaglioppo**. The color alone will make you stop and drink this juicy wine that goes perfectly with the region's fantastic salumi and sheep's milk cheeses.

Dessert

Montonico
A rare white grape that produces excellent dessert wines. Soft and elegant, Montonico produces wines that subtly offer hints of apricots, apples, oranges and even lemon rinds. Hard to find but worth it.

Greco di Bianco
From the seaside town, Bianco, the grapes are semi-dried, so the flavors and high levels of sugars are concentrated.

PUGLIA

Whites :
Locorotondo, Fiano Minutolo

Reds :
Salice Salentino, Primitvo di Manduria, Susumaniello, Uva di Troia

Whites

Locorotondo
Made primarily from the **Verdeca** grape. Usually, nothing exciting, but definitely a summer sipping wine. It is light, high acid, with hints of apricots and nuts. It can be made into serious, age-worthy wines, though, similar to Etna Bianco.

Fiano Minutolo
Fiano Minutolo is not to be confused with Fiano di Avellino. Fiano Minutolo is a very aromatic wine with loads of peach and apricot favors and a touch of floral honey.

Reds

Salice Salentino
This DOC area makes wine produced primarily with the **Negroamaro** grape. Negroamaro translates to "black bitter". It might be an acquired taste, but Salice Salentino is a very dark, deep wine, highly tannic and with hints of dark bitter chocolate and licorice. Great with greens and various pasta dishes.

Primitivo di Manduria
Primitivo is believed by many to be the ancestor of California's Zinfandel grape. Very similar fruit profile, only better balanced. Primitivo has a higher level of acidity with a slightly lower level of fruit. High alcohol with bold dark fruits, Primitivo is a great wine with red meats and heavy pasta dishes.

Susumaniello
Usally belnded with Negroamaro but, on its own, can make plummy, berry-scented wines. Also made into a Rosato.

Uva di Troia
A red grape that is deep colored with high alcohol. Deep pomegranate flavors. The best come from **Castel del Monte**. It makes concentrated wines that are rich and capable of ageing. Also blended to add depth and color. A wine more suitable for red meats.

THE ISLANDS

SICILIA

Whites :
Inzolia, Carricante, Catarratto, Grillo

Reds :
Nero D'Avola, Cerasuolo di Vittoria
Etna Rosso, Faro

Dessert :
Moscato di Pantelleria
Marsala, Malvasie delle Lipari

Whites

Inzolia
Inzolia is typically blended with Trebbiano and Catarratto to form a fresh and lively white with exotic fruit flavors. Good match with seafood. Inzolia is also blended with Grillo to make Marsala.

Carricante
Mostly made on Etna and predominantly featured in **Etna Bianco** blends, Carricante has hints of apples, oranges, anise, and baked apple and, thanks to the volcanic soil of Etna, is minerally, smoky, and flinty. It has very good structure and is actually age worthy. A hard wine to find but very unique and can be quite amazing.

Catarratto
Aromatic grape and Viognier-like.

Grillo
Grillo is refreshing and lively with apple and peach notes and a welcomed nuttiness. Terrrific with any seafood.

Reds

Nero D'Avola
This is THE grape of Sicily. It is dark, soft and quite fruity. It has hints of dark cherries, plums, and blackberries. It can resemble Australian Shiraz, but actually is way better. This grape has high potential if made correctly. Great wine for meat dishes and pasta dishes.

Cerasuolo di Vittoria
Made primarily from **Frappato and Nero D'Avola** grapes. Frappato is a soft and low tannin grape with clear hints of strawberries and cherries. It is blended with Nero D'Avola for extra body and fruit. It's one of the few reds that not only can be served with fish and seafood, but benefits from a few minutes in the fridge to make it slightly cool.

Etna Rosso
The main grape here is **Nerello Mascalese** with smaller amounts of **Nerello Cappuccio**. The Mascalese variety is dark, spicy, and high in alcohol. Etna red wines are also great with roasted meats. It's maybe the only wine that has different personalities. Some can be light and fruity, others are full bodied and funky. I prefer the lighter, Pinot Noir type of Etna Rossos that can rival great, red Burgundies of the same price.

Faro
Faro is very similar to Etna Rosso and made with **Nerello Mascalese, Nerello Cappuccio, and Nocera**.

Dessert

Moscato di Pantelleria
Sometimes, the grapes are dried to produce a very sweet wine. Here, the Moscato is called Zibibbo. Hints of apricots and peaches prevail.

Marsala
Similar to Sherry and Madeira, Marsala can be made dry, semi-sweet, or sweet. Marsala can be either made with **white grapes (Inzolia, Catarratto, Grillo, Damaschino)** or from **red grapes (Perricone, Calabrese---a.k.a. Nero D'Avola, Nerello)**.

Malvasia delle Lipari
Malvasia is all over Italy, but is very well known to produce great apricot and peach scented sweet wine here in Lipari, an island off the coast of Sicily.

SARDEGNA

Whites :
Vermentino, Nuragus, Torbato

Reds :
Cannonau, Monica

Dessert :
Vernaccia di Oristano

Whites

Vermentino
Floral, nutty, herbal, and peachy. Very good in Sardegna and not as herbal as the Vermentino made in Liguria. It has high acidity and matches well with grilled fish.

Nuragus
A light white for sipping or with snacks.

Torbato
Almost faced extinction, like many Italian grapes, but was rescued. Makes dry, medium bodied wines. Highly regarded and worth it if you can find it.

Reds

Cannonau
The Sardinian name for Grenache. Here it provides powerful alcohol levels with ripe flavors and hints of earthiness. Full bodied and very fruity. Blackberries, coffee, and pepper are also noted. Great with hearty meals involving meats, such as roasted pork or lamb.

Monica
Similar to Syrah and the wines made from this grape come across as a rustic Rhône. Monica has lots of fruit, including dark plums and black cherries. It can be smoky, earthy, and, above, all spicy. It has relatively low tannins and low acidity.

Dessert

Vernaccia di Oristano
Not to be confused with the Vernaccia of Tuscany. The Oristano version produces a wine similar to dry aged Oloroso Sherry. The grapes are picked very ripe and are extremely rich in sugar.

LEBANON

Lebanon has a very old culture and has been making wine for thousands of years. Though about 60% of the county is Muslim and, therefore, does not drink alcohol, the remaining 40% are Christians and some of the oldest in the World. Christians have been making great wines in this beautiful country for 2,000 years but, for too long, have been under the radar. Hopefully, this will change. The French were the first to bring their grapes to Lebanon. After their mandate, Lebanon retained some of the French influence. In fact, many Lebanese wineries include the word "Chateau" in their names.

Most wine is produced in the **Beqaa Valley**, the Eastern part of the country.

French red grapes such as the famous Bordeaux varietals **Cabernet Sauvignon** are blended with Rhône grapes like **Carignan, Cinsault, Grenache, and Syrah** with surprising results. On paper, Bordeaux and Rhône don't blend well together but here they do. Lebanon also makes white wine from local grapes like **Obaideh**, which is similar to Chardonnay, and **Merwah**, which is similar to Semillon.

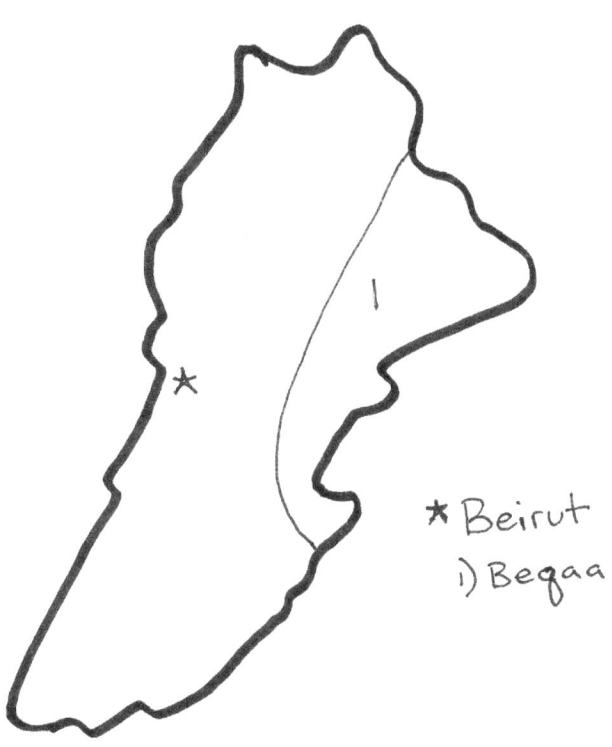

LEBANON

MOROCCO

Morocco has always had close contact with Europe and has had French influence. It's almost all Muslim, so alcohol is forbidden but some good wineries are popping up. Europeans, especially the French, make great wines here.

The 2 best regions for wine are:
Meknès,
with its sub-region, **Coteaux de l'Atlas**
and the
Rabat / Casablanca area,
with its sub-region, **Zenatta**.

Rhône varieties do best in Morocco, with grapes such as **Grenache, Syrah, Carignan, and Cinsault** being made into lush, spicy, and peppery wines.

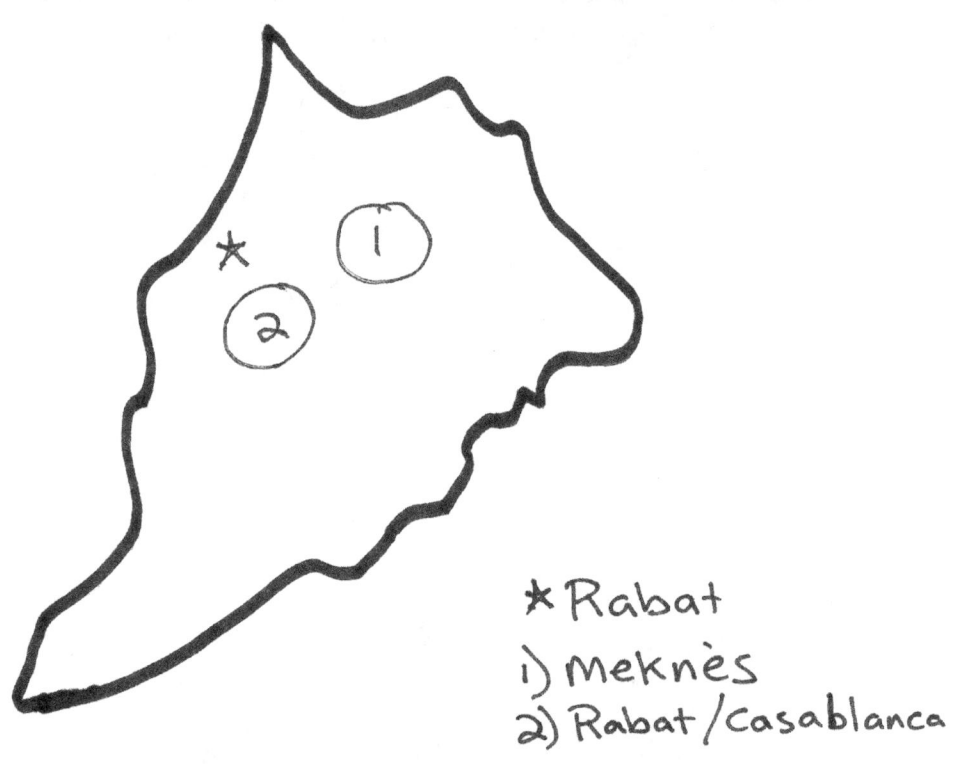

* Rabat
1) Meknès
2) Rabat/Casablanca

MOROCCO

NEW YORK

New York State is the second largest wine producing state; California is #1. New York does well with grapes like **Riesling and Chardonnay**, given its cool weather. It also plants **Cabernet Sauvignon and Pinot Noir** for red. The State makes great **Rosé**, too. The wines can be quite good but quite expensive. Nonetheless, we promote wines of our native State and hope to see them placed among the best in the country.
.

New York State has 3 main wine areas:

Long Island, Hudson River Region, and the Finger Lakes

The Finger Lakes is the state's most important wine region, along with its sub zone **Cayuga Lake**.

Long Island is divided into
North Fork and The Hamptons

★ Albany
1) Cayuga Lake
2) Hudson River Region
3) Long Island

NEW YORK

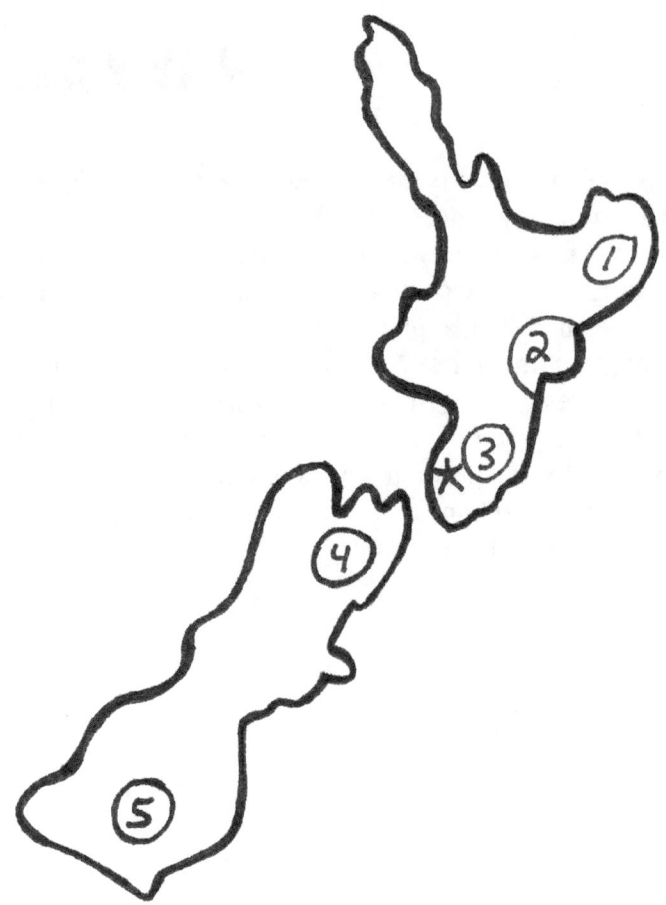

* Wellington
1) Gisborne
2) Hawke's Bay
3) Martinborough
4) Marlborough
5) Central Otago

NEW ZEALAND

NEW ZEALAND

Of all the New World wine countries, I pick New Zealand as my favorite. The whites are considered to be some of the top in the New World. The cool weather climate is perfect for the white Sauvignon Blanc grape. Pinot Noir also happens to do pretty well here. The wines are rarely oaked and the flavors are usually fresh, while maintaining the all-important high level of acidity. New Zealand wines can be a little fruitier than Old World wines, but never as exaggerated as those from California, South America, or Australia. New Zealand got started early on with what took hold in the wine industry. Their aim was to use screw caps instead of corks and they succeeded in being a leader in that movement. However the wines come packaged, New Zealand whites are excellent and you should make sure to try some.

The reds New Zealand produces are typically Pinot Noir and Cabernet. The Pinot Noir can be excellent, while the Cabernets usually display herbal hints, typical when grown in cool weather climates.

Sauvignon Blanc
If you are looking for Sauvignon Blanc, there is no shortage here. The top wine area for this grape is **Marlborough**. The wines have the typical hints of herbs but also display exotic fruits as well a citrus. Can easily pair with most vegetables, even the impossible asparagus and artichoke. Great with an array of fish. Try it with pasta with pesto.

Chardonnay
The two places for New Zealand Chardonnay are **Hawke's Bay and Gisborne**. The Chardonnays here can be some of the best of all New World whites. If they are oaked, it is done minimally. Higher acidity than anything from California. Great with shellfish and fish. A great white for cream-based dishes.

Pinot Noir
The cool weather of both **Martinborough and Central Otago** is perfect for Burgundy's Pinot Noir grape. Very versatile wines that match great with chicken, pork, and also veal.

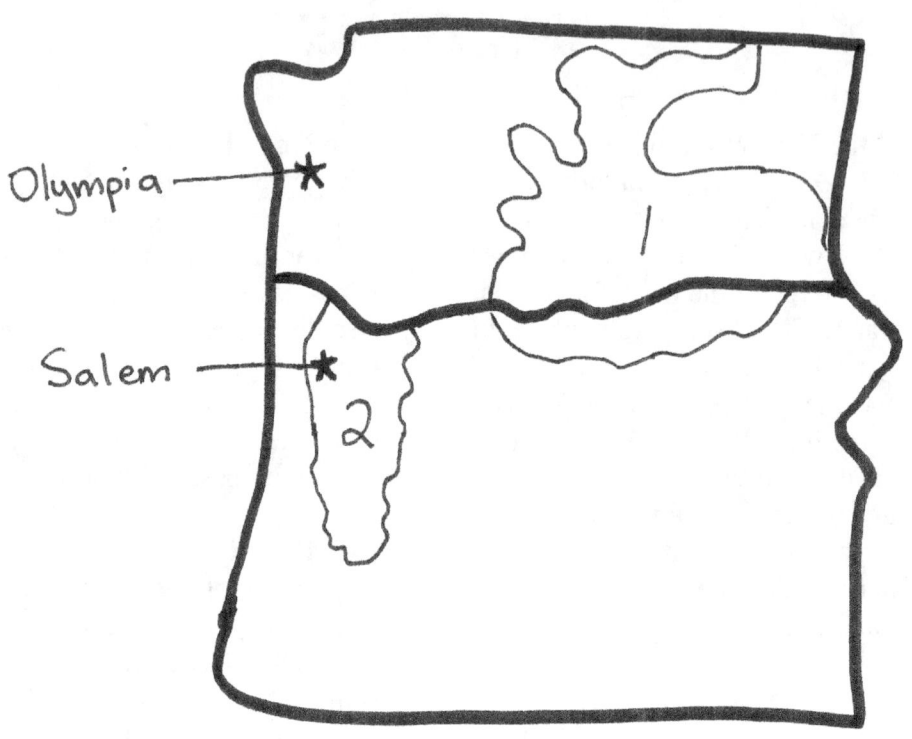

1) Columbia Valley
2) Williamette Valley

OREGON
and
WASHINGTON

OREGON

Part of what is known as the Pacific Northwest, Oregon can produce really good **Pinot Noir**. It also makes good **Pinot Gris, Riesling, and Chardonnay**. The cool weather limits the variety of grapes that can be planted and, in this case, that's a good thing.

Oregon, as well as Washington, focuses on only a few grapes and sticks with them. Oregon rarely mimics California's tendency to follow trends. The main wine you will find from Oregon is red made from Pinot Noir.

Williamette Valley

THE place for Oregon **Pinot Noir**. The grape is hard to grow, so expect to pay a substantial amount for good Pinot Noir. For $20 - $30, you can find a good bottle displaying hints of cherries and raspberries, strawberries, and spice. For over $ 40, you get amazing Pinot Noir. The wines do have good acidity, although some producers ruin it by ageing it too long in oak barrels. Great match with chicken, pork, turkey, and vegetable dishes.

WASHINGTON STATE

The other portion of the Pacific Northwest, Washington State has even cooler weather than Oregon. It produces mostly **Chardonnay, Cabernet, and Merlot**.

Columbia Valley is the main wine area with two sub regions:

Walla Walla Valley
Yakima Valley

The **Merlots** from Washington State are considered the best in the U.S.A. Yes, that's right, better than California Merlots. Although New World in style, it is not as big, over ripe, and clumsy as California Merlot. Washington's Merlots are full bodied with better acidity than the ones from California and, hence, much better with food. The Cabernet Sauvignons can also be very good and are much better with food than California wines.

★ Lisbon
1) Vinho Verde
2) Douro
3) Port
4) Bairrada
5) Dao
6) Colares
7) Madeira

PORTUGAL

PORTUGAL

Quick, what's the first thing that comes to mind when you think Portuguese wine? Most likely you would answer Port. Port definitely is this country's most famous product, but Portugal also produces red and white wine. For very long, if it wasn't Port, nobody cared. But now people are staring to care. Portugal, like most European countries, is soaked in tradition. This can be a double-edged sword. Old ways of doing things had left Portugal's wine quality in the dark. Producers started to realize what works best for certain grapes to make certain wines. Newer, improved techniques are now being used. Careful attention is being given to grape yields and vinification methods.

Portugal is planning to keep it smart. They are strong believers in using indigenous grapes to represent their country on the world wine stage. Red and white wines, in my opinion, will never replace the importance and quality of Port. Portugal *is* Port and will most likely remain so. It is their country's pride and joy. Portuguese wines go best with Portuguese food. The wines are simple and rustic, like the great food and kind people.

The better wine producing regions are located in the north. The more important wine regions are broken down geographically as such:

NORTH : Bairrada, Dao, Douro, Vinho Verde, Port

CENTRAL : Colares

ISLAND : Madeira

NORTH

Bairrada

Bairrada produces mostly red wine made primarily from a grape called **Baga**. Smaller amounts of **Periquita, Bastardo, and Tinta Pinheira** are also included. The Bairrada reds are wines that need to age for quite a while. They have a lot of tannins and high acidity. Known as Portugal's top red wine region. Producers are trying to tame the rough tannins and soften the wine up as a whole. The newer wines are a little more fruit driven, but still considered big, tannic, and acidic. The wine is well suited for red meat dishes.

Dao

Dao produces mostly red wine. They are very big and considered quite rough. These full bodied reds need time to soften. Quite popular wine region, although not on the same level of quality as the Bairrada wines. The main grapes are **Alfrocheiro, Preto, Bastardo, and Touriga Nacional**. The wines can be spicy with hints of forest fruits.

Douro

The Douro region actually has two major wine producing areas: Douro and Port. I have dedicated a section just for Port, but here I wish to discuss the reds and whites of just Douro. The reds and whites of the Douro are often pushed aside for the world popular Port. The reds are blends of **Tinta Roriz** (Tempranillo in Spain) and **Touriga Nacional**. For the whites, **Verdelho** is the main grape. Verdelho may be Spain's Godello grape.

Vinho Verde

Vinho Verde literally means green wine. The word green is meant to describe the wine's freshness and youthfulness, not its color. Vinho Verde can be red or white, with the white being much better. The white Vinho Verde is made primarily from **Alvarinho** (Albariño in Spain). The wines are usually very dry and crisp (high acidity). They are also typically slightly effervescent. These qualities make Vinho Verde the perfect summer sipping wine. It is also great with shellfish and light snacks or as an aperitif.

Port

Portugal's most famous export is a sweet fortified wine. Ports may be white or red, however, it is the red Port that conquers hearts and imaginations. The main grapes for red Port are **Tinta Barocca, Tinta Cao, Tinta Roriz (Tempranillo in Spain), Touriga Nacional, and Touriga Francesa**.

Halfway through the fermentation process, extra alcohol is added. This addition stops the fermentation process, leaving the wine with a lot of sugar that has not turned into alcohol. This extra sugar is called residual sugar. The result is a wine with a higher level of alcohol and sugar. The wine is then aged before its release. Port is one of the best options for after dinner. It is also a stunning match with blue cheeses like Roquefort or Gorgonzola. Some enjoy Port with fruits like strawberries. You will usually see some Ports with English names. Englishmen in Portugal created most of the Port companies and so named the companies after themselves.

There are many kinds of Port, but there are 3 main categories: ***Ruby Port, Tawny Port, Vintage Port***

Ruby Port

Ruby Ports are essentially Port wines made from lower quality batches. It is aged and then released. These are typically fruity with a light red color. Meant to be drunk young. Not considered anything great, so prices remain low.

Tawny Port

Tawny Ports are like the next step up (actually way, way up). They are made by combining blends of wines from different years. They are typically aged before release. They are called Tawny Ports because they are tawny in color. Cheaper Tawny Ports are sometimes made, which are essentially blends of White Port and Ruby Port. Forget this one and go straight for the Tawny Ports. These wines are sometimes aged 10, 20, 30, or even 40 years.

Vintage Port

The best and most expensive of all Ports. Only the grapes from a single vintage are used. These grape are the best picks of all the batches and come from specially selected sites. It is also made only in the best vintages. A Port producer does not make Vintage Port every year. Remember, they must be from the best years or else there will be NO Vintage Port made. These Ports can age up to an astounding 50 years.

When I say "Vintage", it can be misleading. Vintage only denotes quality when it applies to Champagne or Port.

These two wines use the word vintage to imply the wine from a certain year has been declared extraordinary and exceptional. In any other case, the word vintage is not meant to imply that the wine is either good or bad.

There are also a few kinds of Vintage Port:

Single-Quinta Port,
Second Label Vintage Port
Late-Bottled Vintage Port
Colheita Port

Single-Quinta Port
A less intense Vintage Port with less fullness and richness.

Second Label Vintage Port
If a Port company does not feel that a vintage year should be declared, they bottle the wine as Second Label Port. The wines missed being declared completely Vintage but are of amazing quality nonetheless.

Late-Bottled Vintage Port
Made from the grapes of a single vintage, not a blend of different years, but the level of quality is not as high as the ones labeled simply Vintage. Also called LBV, it is considered like a high quality Ruby Port. Late bottled Vintage Ports cannot age as well as Vintage Ports. Drink early.

Colheita Port
Essentially the same as a Late-Bottled Vintage Port, but Colheita Port is aged longer considered to be more of a Tawny Port than a Ruby Port.

CENTRAL

Colares
Colares is mainly known for its red wine made from grapes like **Ramisco, Periquita, and Molar**, among others. The wines are very tannic and need time to soften up. The full-bodied wines of this area need ageing, as some people may find the amount of tannins excessive and unbearable.

ISLAND

Madeira
Forget the Madeira made in the States, which is a pathetic copy of the original. Real Madeira, made from red **Negra Mole** grapes, comes from the Island of Madeira. The wines are exposed to heat and oxidation. The resulting wines may be very dry to even sweet. Considered one of the top fortified wines, along with Port and Sherry.

SLOVENIA

Bordering Italy's north-eastern tip, Slovenia has a lot of potential for great wine, especially for its white wines.

It has 3 main wine regions :

Primorska, Posavska, Podravska.

Podravksa makes the most, in terms of quantity. The best region for white is Primorska and does well with Italian varieties, especially **Rebula**, the Italia Ribolla Gialla grape. The Primorska region is very similar to the Italian Friuli region.

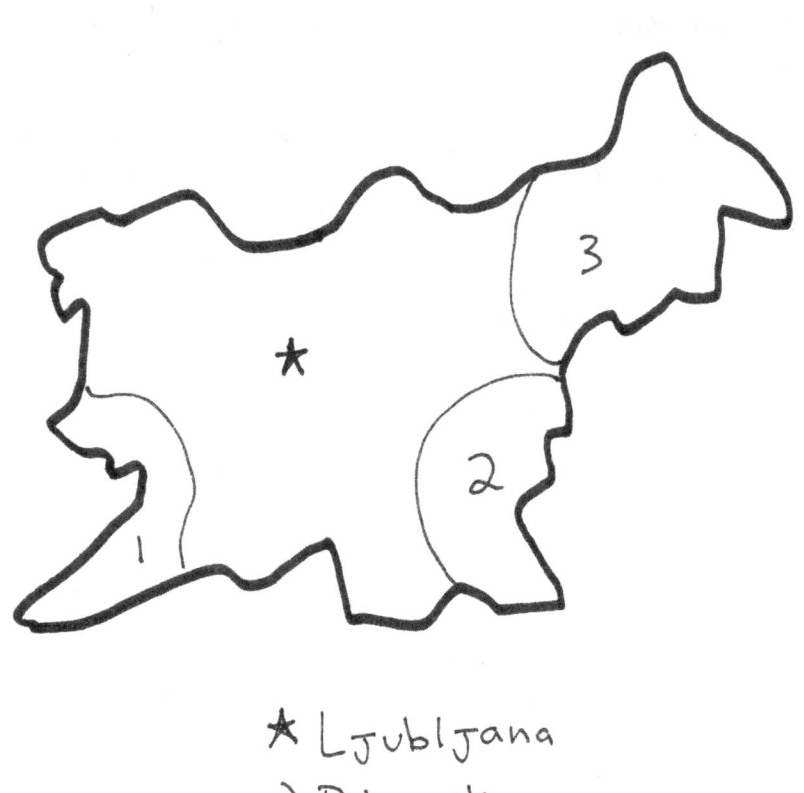

★ Ljubljana
1) Primorska
2) Posavska
3) Podravska

SLOVENIA

SOUTH AFRICA

South Africa is up and coming. It makes reds and whites all from European grapes. **Chardonnay, Sauvignon Blanc, Chenin Blanc, Cabernet, Merlot, and Shiraz** are all planted here.

The reds, however, are what gain international attention. South Africa is famous for a grape called Pinotage. **Pinotage** is a cross between Pinot Noir and Cinsault, which the South Africans call Hermitage and, thus, the name Pinotage.

The main wine areas to know are:

Stellenbosch
Swartland
Constantia
Paarl

South African Merlots and Cabernets best represent this country on the world's wine stage. The abundant sunshine lets South Africa harvest ripe grapes full of fruit and body. The reds such as Shiraz, Cabernet, and Merlot all go best with red meat.

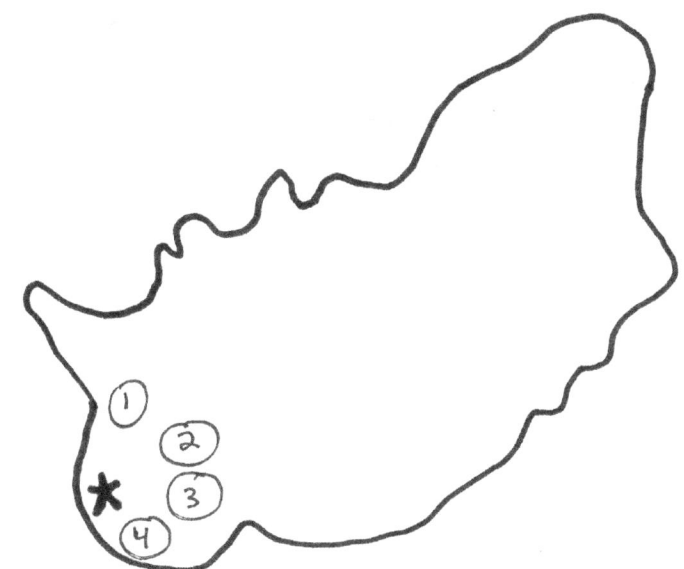

★ Capetown
1) Swartland
2) Paarl
3) Stellenbosch
4) Constantia

SOUTH AFRICA

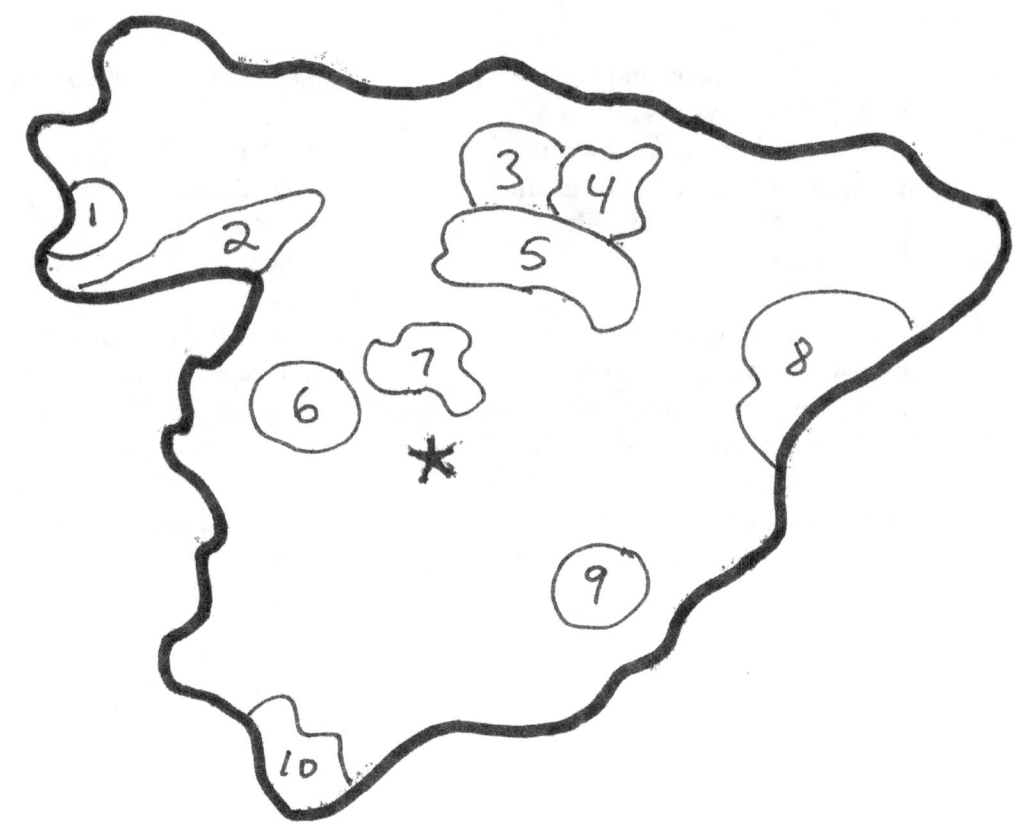

★ Madrid
1) Rias Biaxas
2) Ribeiro
3) Basque
4) Navarra
5) Rioja
6) Rueda
7) Ribera del Duero
8) Catalonia
9) Jumilla
10) Jerez

SPAIN

SPAIN

Spain, for most of its history, has never been world renown for wine quality, although it plays a very important role in Spanish life. The image and reputation of Spanish wine has been changing for the better since the 1990's. For long, Spain has been closely associated with Sherry, and pretty much nothing else. However, today, people are paying closer attention to newer, more exciting red and white wines coming out of Spain.

Spanish wine mirrors its culture, landscape, and people. Her wines are rustic and satisfying. The international varieties have invaded and taken over, but there are numerous good wines from indigenous grapes to be found. The international varieties seem to do very well when blended with Spain's indigenous grapes. Cabernet Sauvignon is typically blended with Spain's red Tempranillo grape. The results can be excellent.

I must mention that in Spain, as everywhere else, there are a few rotten apples. Some producers feel the urgent need to make new, fashionable style wines. The result is a bunch of Spanish wines that all taste alike. Overoaked, overripe, and over everything for that matter. These wines should be overlooked. Some producers are trying too hard to conform to new wine trends. We could all send a message to these people by not buying their wines. They will then be forced to make better (real), more food friendly wine. Spanish wine goes best with Spanish food. This combination should not be sacrificed for the sake of jumping on the bandwagon.

This is not to say that the bulk of bad Spanish wine is the fault of those wanna-be groupie, wine producers. Spanish wine in general was suffering for a while. Rules and regulations were lax and people seemed not to care. Many Spanish grapes are only capable of producing ordinary, low acid wines with excessively high alcohol and no balance. Smart producers are now paying close attention to how to maximize the potential of Spanish wine and emphasize the grapes' positive features rather than its flaws. Stick to Spanish wines that speak of the land, history, and culture. Those are great!

There are many wine producing regions in Spain.
The main 10 you should know are divided geographically.

NORTHWEST :
Rias Biaxas, Ribeiro

NORTH :
Navarra, Rioja, Ribera del Duero, Rueda

NORTHEAST :
Catalonia, Basque Country

SOUTHWEST :
Jerez

SOUTHEAST :
Jumilla

NORTHWEST

Rias Biaxas

Albariño
This white grape is very thick-skinned and, therefore, produces very little juice. The resulting juice is usually of very good quality. It is very aromatic and compared to Viognier and Gewurztraminer. It is lighter than the two with hints of peaches, apricots, and its trademark characteristic of citrus. It has good acidity and, therefore, is food friendly. Good Albariño can be expensive, but worth the money. Perfect for shellfish, fish, white meats, appetizers, and even as an aperitif.

Ribeiro

Palomino
Possibly one of the most worthless grapes for producing wine, in this case white wines. Totally a waste of time, UNLESS it is planted much further south where it is used to make the famous and stunning Sherries of the world. Unfortunately, here in the Northwest, it is the most planted junk around. Fortunately, producers are realizing it is only good for Sherry and are planting the much, much better Godello.

Godello
Northwest Spain has been waking up to Godello. What a relief! And it is about time. Producers are ripping out those crappy Palomino vines and are now planting Godello. Godello has nice hints of apricots and peaches. Not as good as Albariño, but close. These wines are compared to Portugal's Vinho Verde.

NORTH

Navarra
A wine region noted for nothing great, except its great rosé wines, called **Rosado**, typically made from **Garnacha** (Grenache in French) grapes and Tempranillo. Navarra Rosados are great, inexpensive values. You can do no wrong with these wines.

Rioja
Rioja has long represented the epitome of Spanish wine. It is Spain at its core. Riojas have taken their place on the world stage and rightfully so. Rioja *is* red wine. The whites are mediocre, at best. The main red grape is **Tempranillo**. Smaller amounts of **Garnacha, Carignan, and Graciano** may be added. Tempranillo can be medium to full bodied with hints of strawberries, raspberries, black berries, black cherries, and, of course, tobacco. Better drunk early. Great with pork and pork products. Match Rioja with poultry and other light meats.

Ribera del Duero
Ribera del Duero is proving to be a top contender as one of Spain's top reds; the whites are insignificant. The red grape most widely used is **Tempranillo**. The Tempranillos here differ from the Riojas in the sense that they are darker and more age worthy. As Ribera del Duero wines age, they exhibit dark plums and prunes. Bitter chocolate and, of course, tobacco are also present. These wines are typically quite rough. Drink Riojas earlier and save the Ribera del Dueros for later.

Rueda

The only wine region in northern Spain that makes really good white wine. Reds are nothing of importance. Rueda wines primarily blend white grapes such as **Verdejo and Viura**. The international white grape **Sauvignon Blanc** does exceptionally well here. Rueda wines can have hints of pears and grapefruit. If Sauvignon Blanc is added, then Ruedas become more exciting, with better acidity and hints of dried herbs. Great wine for fish.

NORTHEAST

Catalonia

The main 2 wine areas are:
Penèdes, Priorato

Penèdes

Penèdes makes mostly white wine. Its whites are usually blends of grapes such as **Parellada, Macabeo, and Xarel-lo**. **Chardonna**y has now become very popular in Penèdes and is used in the blends. The whites are pretty average and should be drunk as young as possible. These whites are also made into **Cava**, which is Spain's answer to Champagne. This Spanish sparkler is produced all over the north of Spain, but mostly concentrated in Penèdes, specifically the area of Cava. Cava Sparklers are never really anything special. The Penèdes region produces small amounts of red wine primarily from Garnacha, while Cabernet Sauvignon producing Penèdes' best red.

Priorato

Priorato is known strictly for its red wine, which is considered one of the best in Spain. Prioratos are hard to come by and quite expensive. It rushed onto the world's wine stage and it looks like it is here to stay, and that's a good thing. The main grape is **Garnacha**. Older Prioratos were very big, black, and alcoholic. They aged forever and were ready for consumption years after its release. New producers are making these wines a little more accessible. They may even blend Cabernet Sauvignon or Merlot. Priorato reds can have hints of black cherries, figs, spice, tar, and even leather. High alcohol and meant to go with red meat. It is also spelled without the final o : Priorat.

BASQUE COUNTRY

It probably would bother a native of Basque Country to have the region stuck in Spain and it would bother the Spaniard that I would say Basque wines are some of my favorite from Spain, but there's nothing I can do about it. Basque wines are very intriguing. They are mostly from **Txakoli** and can be made into a spritzy white, made from **Hondaribbi Zuri**, with mineral hints of tropical fruits and a solid backbone of salinity. The reds are made from **Hondarrabi Beltza**, which is similar to Cabernet Franc but much more fun. It can boast dark fruits like blackberries, dark cherries, and plum, with a peppery frame.

SOUTHWEST

Jerez

The motherland of Sherry. Sherry is a fortified wine made primarily from the white **Palomino** grape. There are 2 kinds of Sherry: **Fino and Oloroso**. The difference between the two is something called *flor*. Flor is a kind of yeast that is naturally present ONLY in Fino Sherries. Fino Sherry is lower in alcohol and therefore allows the flor to develop. Oloroso Sherry is too high in alcohol to allow flor to develop. The Sherry is aged in wood barrels but only filled about 80%. The other 20% gives room for the flor to develop (only in Fino Sherries). The flor eliminates exposure to oxygen and, therefore, prevents oxidation. The flor is what gives Fino Sherries their tangy and pungent characteristics. Fino does not age well. When it does age, it loses its flor. The Sherry then changes into an amber color and starts to taste a little nutty, similar to Oloroso. This is labeled a Fino Amontillado. If the Sherry is aged longer and is softer and darker, it is then labeled simply Amontillado. Of all the Fino style Sherries, the lightest and most pungent of all is called Manzanilla. Fino Sherries are considered to be the best of all Sherries.

Oloroso Sherry does not use and develop the flor. Without flor, Oloroso Sherry is prone to oxidation. This exposure to air is what gives Oloroso Sherry its characteristic, dark brown color and nutty/raisiny taste. Olorosos are aged longer and are pretty high in alcohol.

Oloroso Sherry is best served between 56 – 60 degrees Fahrenheit.

Fino Sherries can be served chilled between 48 – 52 degrees Fahrenheit.

SOUTHEAST

Jumilla

Jumilla is an up and coming wine region. It historically produced average wines that were unbearably high in alcohol. New producers are now picking the grapes earlier to avoid high sugar content and, therefore, high alcohol. The main grape is **Monastrell**. Monastrell is the Spanish name for Mourvèdre. The wine is blended occasionally with small amounts of Tempranillo or Garnacha. International varieties like Cabernet Sauvignon and Merlot are also now being added. High in alcohol and low in acid, Jumilla wines have typical hints of blackberries and spice.

* Bern
1) French Switzerland
2) German Switzerland
3) Italian Switzerland

SWITZERLAND

SWITZERLAND

Switzerland is an interesting country and has an even more interesting culture. Or should I say cultures, plural? It has Italy to the south, Germany to the north, France to the west, and Austria and Liechtenstein to the east. There are 4 languages spoken, which are, in order of percentage of native-speakers, German, French, Italian, and Romansh. Switzerland is divided into 26 cantons, like our 50 states in America, and visualized in German Switzerland, French Switzerland, and Italian Switzerland, all listed in order of size. The cultures feed off each other to produce a dynamic society. The country is known for banking, chocolate, and efficiency, but wine? Almost all Swiss wines never leave the country! That's too bad because they have some good ones.

When thinking of Swiss wines, it would make sense to think of them as similar to German ones and maybe a little French. They are but don't taste as crisp as German and French, particularly, Alsatian. Many Swiss producers prefer malolactic fermentation to soften the acidity. Generally, I am against this for whites but, given Switzerland's climate, the grapes are high in acidity anyway, so, in this case, malolactic fermentation could be welcomed.

Swiss wine regions are essentially divided into :

French Switzerland
German Switzerland
Italian Switzerland

French Switzerland
The **Valais** is the most important region in all of the country; **Vaud** is second. **Petite Arvine, Chasselas, and Malvoise (Pinot Gris)** are mostly used for white wines. For reds, **Cornalin, Pinot Noir, and Gamay** are very common.

German Switzerland
For whites, **Muller Thurgau, Gruner Veltliner, and Riesling** are mostly used. **Pinot Noir** is the most common red made here.

Italy Switzerland
For some odd reason, almost all grapes planted here are **Merlot**.

TURKEY

Turkey is a very large country with an ancient wine history. The Greeks and the Romans made wine here. Though it is predominantly a Muslim country, where alcohol is not consumed, most Turks are secular when it comes to wine. Though it is so large that it covers two continents (Europe and Asia), there are only 2 main wine regions to note. The Aegean and Marmara regions offer hope for this country's wine industry.

The **Aegean** wine region is the most productive and where the best wines are found. International varieties do well here, such as **Cabernet, Merlot, Syrah, and Grenache**.

The **Marmara** wine region is considered second best with international varieties and some interesting white wine production.

★ Ankara

1) Marmara
2) Aegean

TURKEY

URUGUAY

Canelones is the biggest and best region for wine in Uruguay and one wine comes to mind when mentioning Uruguay : Tannat. **Tannat** is to Uruguay what Malbec is to Argentina. Both Malbec and Tannat come from southern France and do well in these South American countries. If you like the dark, meaty profile of Malbec but want an even darker and funkier version, Tannat is for you. Excellent with any meat.

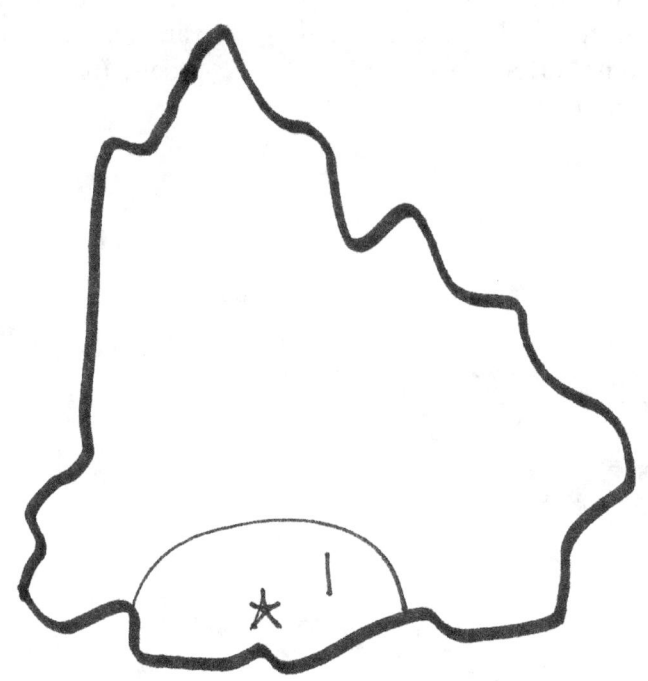

★ Montevideo
1) Canelones

URUGUAY

MATCHING WINE WITH FOOD

The age old trick has always been white with fish and red with meat. While that may be true, it gets much more complicated than that. Nowadays, some people believe you should drink whatever you like with whatever you eat. You can do that, but you would be making more than a few mistakes. You are entitled to drink whatever you choose, but remember there are undeniable matches and mismatches when it comes to food and wine. Before getting into it a little more specifically, I wish to offer a few helpful guidelines.

Pair Body Weights
Light bodied wines go best with lighter dishes. Heavy dishes go best with heavier wines. A plate of grilled chicken and mashed potatoes would be overshadowed if paired with the typically humongous Amarone. You would do better with a Chablis.

Yin and Yang
A good tip is to balance opposites or extremes. If you were eating something salty and spicy, then a nice juicy and sweeter Riesling would be appropriate. For a cream based dish, a nice acidic wine can help cut the richness.

Do the Same
If you are eating a peppery steak, a nice compliment would be the peppery and spicy Rhône wines or other Syrah based wines. If a dish consists of roasted herbs, an herbaceous Sauvignon Blanc would do the trick.

When in Rome, Do as the Romans do (LITERALLY)
When pairing wine with certain cuisines, make it a habit to pair a wine made in the same region where the food is popular. Nothing marries better than the famous goat cheese from the Loire and her equally famous Sancerre (Sauvignon Blanc). This regional food and regional wine combination is nowhere better exemplified than in Italy. The food and wine tradition is older, more extensive, and more closely linked than those of any other country.

SOME DO'S AND DON'TS

1) Wine with salad is almost always a no-no. The vinegar ruins everything. I usually take a break when eating my salad and just drink water.

2) Red wine can taste metallic with many kinds of fish. The only reds I would ever pair with fish are Pinot Noir, Beaujolais, Etna Rosso, Schiava, and very few others.

3) Salty foods cry for sweeter wines to create a harmonious balance.

4) The spicier the food, the lower alcohol the wine should have. High alcohol and spice give a hot taste in the mouth.

5) Tannic red wines need red meat and vice versa. The fat helps soften the tannins, while the tannins help tackle a big dish like steak.

6) Asian cuisines such as Thai, Vietnamese, and Indian use many different spices. The main wines are Riesling and Vouvray for whites and Beaujolais and Cabernet Franc for reds.

Here is a list of the most popular dishes in America and the wines to accompany them

GENERAL APPETIZERS

Whites
Muscadet, Sancerre, Champagne, Vouvray, Picpoul, German Riesling Kabinett, Gruner, Vinho Verde, Moscato D'Asti, Franciacorta, Prosecco, Soave, Kerner, Gavi, Pinot Grigio, Greco di Tufo, Falanghina, Vernaccia, Orvieto, Vermentino, Santorini, Sauvignon Blanc, Torrontés

Rosé
Provence, Languedoc- Roussillon, Navarra Rosado, Cirò Rosato, Cerasuolo d'Abruzzo

Reds
Pinot Noir, Beaujolais, Rioja, Primitivo, Nero d'Avola, Schiava, Montepulciano d'Abruzzo

PASTA

Tomato Sauce

Reds
Barbera, Nebbiolo d'Alba, Valpolicella, Ripasso, Chianti, Vino Nobile di Montepulciano, Salice Salentino, Aglianico

Garlic and Oil

Whites
Greco di Tufo, Falanghina, Gavi

Rosato
Cerasuolo

Reds
Chianti, Dolcetto, Barbera, Valpolicella

Pesto

Whites
Arneis, Sauvignon Blanc, Ribolla Gialla, Tocai Friulano, Greco di Tufo, Pigato, Vermentino, Gavi

Eggplant

Reds
Nero d'Avola, Cirò, Primitivo, Taurasi, Rosso Piceno, Aglianico, Etna Rosso, Cerasuolo di Vittoria, Monica, Cannonau

Mushrooms

Reds
Chianti, Dolcetto, Barbera, Valpolicella, Cabernet Franc, Lagrein Dunkel, Ruchè, Freisa, Pelaverga, Grignolino, Schiava

Pumpkin

Reds
Nero, d'Avola, Ripasso, Valpolicella, Dolcetto, Salice Salentino, Gutturnio

Beans

Reds
Chianti, Montepulciano d'Abruzzo, Vino Nobile di Montepulciano, Rosso Conero, Morellino di Scansano, Pugnitello, Cesanese

Broccoli

Whites
Arneis, Fiano di Avellino, Greco di Tufo, Soave

Reds
Salice Salentino, Primitivo, Cirò Rosso

Cream Sauces

Whites
Tocai Friulano, Ribolla Gialla, Pinot Grigio, Soave, Gavi, Albana, Kerner

Reds
Valpolicella, Chianti, Montepulciano d'Abruzzo

Lasagne and stuffed Pastas

Reds
Nebbiolo d'Alba, Boca, Gattinara, Barbaresco, Barolo, Ripasso, Amarone, Refosco, Pignolo, Gutturnio, Schioppetino, Rosso di Montalcino, Brunello di Montalcino, Super Tuscan, Vino Nobile di Montepucliano, Chianti, Sagrantino, Taurasi, Aglianico del Vulture, Nero D'Avola, Salice Salentino, Cannonau

Meat Sauces

Reds
Nebbiolo d'Alba, Boca, Gattinara, Barbaresco, Barolo, Ripasso, Amarone, Refosco, Pignolo, Gutturnio, Schioppetino, Rosso di Montalcino, Brunello di Montalcino, Super Tuscan, Vino Nobile di Montepulciano, Chianti, Sagrantino, Taurasi, Aglianico del Vulture, Nero D'Avola, Salice Salentino, Cannonau

Shellfish

Whites

Verdicchio, Arneis, Erbaluce, Gavi, Pigato, Vermentino, Blanc de Morgex et de La Salle, Prosecco, Vespaiola, Tocai Friulano, Ribolla Gialla, Pinot Grigio, Soave, Lugana, Kerner, Passerina, Pecorino, Cococciola, Greco di Tufo, Fiano di Avellino, Coda di Volpe, Ischia Bianco, Ravello Bianco, Pallagrello Bianco, Cirò Bianco, Etna Bianco, Grillo, Inzolia, Catarratto

Rosato
Cirò, Cerasuolo

RISOTTO

Alla Milanese

Whites
Tocai Friulano,
Ribolla Giallo,
Fiano di Avellino

Reds
Oltrepò Pavese,
Valpolicella, Ripasso,
Nebbiolo d'Alba,
Barbaresco, Barolo,
Lessona, Bramaterra,
Valtellina

Vegetables

Whites
Tocai Friulano,
Ribolla Gialla, Arneis,
Sauvignon Blanc

Red
Pinot Noir,
Valpolicella, Chianti

Truffles

Whites
Timorasso,
Blanc de Morgex et de
la Salle, Kerner

Reds
Barolo, Barbaresco,
Gattinara, Valtellina,
Sagrantino, Taurasi

Shellfish

Whites
Verdicchio, Arneis, Greco di Tufo,
Falanghina, Fiano di Avellino,
Coda di Volpe, Ischia,
Pallagrello Bianco, Cirò Bianco,
Etna Bianco, Prosecco, Soave,
Tocai Friulano, Ribolla Gialla, Kerner,
Pigato, Vermentino, Passerina,
Pecorino, Cococciola

Meat

Reds
Nebbiolo d'Alba, Boca, Gattinara,
Barbaresco, Barolo, Ripasso, Amarone,
Refosco, Pignolo, Gutturnio,
Schioppetino,
Rosso di Montalcino,
Brunello di Montalcino, Super Tuscan,
Vino Nobile di Montepucliano, Chianti,
Sagrantino, Taurasi,
Aglianico del Vulture, Nero D'Avola,
Salice Salentino, Cannonau

PIZZA

Whites
Greco di Tufo, Falanghina, Fiano di Avellino, Coda di Volpe, Ischia, Pallagrello Bianco, Cirò Bianco, Etna Bianco, Kerner, Cocacciola

Rosato
Cirò, Etna Rosato, Cerasuolo

Reds
Gragnano, Aglianico, Barbera, Dolcetto, Chianti, Nero D'Avola, Primitivo, Lacrima di Morro D'Alba, Malbec, Lambrusco

FISH

Light Fish Such As:
Flounder, Sole, Trout, Bass, Red Mullet, and Fluke

White

New Zealand Sauvignon Blanc, Sancerre, Chablis, Rieslings, Greco di Tufo,

Fiano di Avellino, Falanghina, Prosecco, Tocai Friulano, Ribolla Gialla, Pinot Grigio, Gavi, Pecorino,

Passerina, Pigato, Vermentino, Blanc de Morgex et de La Salle, Kerner, Verdicchio

Fatty / Oily Fish
Such As: Salmon, Blue Fish, Tuna, Swordfish, and Mackerel, etc

Whites
Meursault, Montrachet, Chablis, Alsace Riesling, Alsace Gewurztraminer, Gruner Veltliner, Viognier, Albariño, Etna Bianco
Greco di Tufo, Fiano di Avellino, Erbaluce

Reds
Pinot Noir, Cerasuolo di Vittoria, Etna Rosso

SUSHI, SASHIMI, AND POKE

Whites
German Riesling, Picpoul, Kerner, Tocai Friulano

Rosé
Provence
Languedoc-Roussillon

Reds
Pinot Noir
Cerasuolo di Vittoria
Schiava

Seafood Teriyaki

Whites
Spatlese Riesling
Vouvray

Salmon Teriyaki

Whites
Champagne, Prosecco

Shellfish

Whites
Verdicchio, Soave,
Ribolla Gialla, Tocai
Friulano. Pinot Grigio,
Greco di Tufo
Falanghina, Albariño,
Vinho Verde, Vouvray
German Riesling
Gruner Veltliner,
Prosecco, Champagne

CEVICHE
Whites
Prosecco
Champagne

SMOKED FISH / CAVIAR

Champagne with these two may be the most common option but is not nearly the perfect match. As much as I hate vodka, it would be your best choice.
Or Riesling

POULTRY

Rotisserie Chicken

Whites
Sauvignon Blanc
California Chardonnay

Reds
Pinot Noir
Cabernet Franc, Rioja

Chicken Cutlet

Whites
Tocai Friulano
Pinot Grigio

Reds
Barbera, Nero D'Avola

Chicken Teriyaki

Reds
Beaujolais
Cabernet Franc

Mole Poblano

Reds
Côtes du Rhône
Cabernet Franc

Tacos / Burritos

Reds
Côtes du Rhône
Cabernet Franc
Nero d'Avola, Shiraz

Chicken Szechuan

Whites
Riesling, Moscato d'Asti

Reds
Beaujolais, Cab Franc

Barbecued Chicken

Reds
Chilean Cabernet

Fried Chicken

Whites
New Zealand Sauvignon Blanc, California Chardonnay

Reds
Chilean Cabernet

Chicken Vindaloo

Whites
German Rieslings
Gewurztraminer
Gruner Veltliner

Chicken Saag

Whites
Sauvignon Blanc
Vouvray

Reds
Rioja

Thanksgiving Turkey

Whites
Viognier German Rieslings California Chardonnay

Reds
Zinfandel
Primitivo
Ripasso

Braised Rabbit

Whites
Ischia Bianco
German Rieslings

Reds
Valpolicella
Salice Salentino
Burgundy Pinot Noir
Orgeon Pinot Noir

Duck / Goose Foie Gras

Whites
German Riesling, Alsace Pinot Gris
Sauternes

Reds
Pinot Noir
Etna Rosso

PORK

Pork Chops

Whites
German Riesling
Alsace Riesling
Alsace Pinot Gris
Alsace Gewurztraminer
Gruner Veltliner

Reds
Pinot Noir
Etna Rosso

Braciola

Reds
Valpolicella
Ripasso
Nebbiolo d'Alba
Barbaresco, Cirò Rosso
Taurasi, Aglianico,
Nero d'Avola
Etna Rosso

Charcuterie

Whites
Sancerre, Greco di Tufo
Gruner Veltliner

Reds
German Pinot Noir
Cabernet Franc

Choucroute Garni

Whites
Alsace Pinot Gris
Gewurztraminer
Gruner Veltliner

Reds
German Pinot Noir
Rioja

Barbecued Ribs

Reds
Australian Shiraz
Chilean Cabernet

Ham

Rosé
Rosé d'Anjou
Navarra Rosado
Lagrein Kretzer
Cirò Rosato

Reds
German Pinot Noir
Lagrein Dunkel
Zweigelt, Schiava

Sausage

Whites
Greco di Tufo
Gewurztraminer, Gruner
Veltliner, Albariño

Reds
Côtes du Rhône
Australian Shiraz
Nemea, Rioja
Primitivo, Douro

Salami

Whites
Rieslings, Viognier,
Gewurztraminer,
Pinot Bianco, Kerner
Fiano di Avellino
Greco di Tufo
Cirò Bianco

Rosato
Cirò Rosato
Cerasuolo d'Abruzzo

Reds
Montepulciano
d'Abruzzo, Cirò Rosso
German Pinot Noir

Cured Pork Products Such as : Prosciutto, Culatello, Mortadella, Speck, Iberico, Serrano

Whites
Tocai Friulano
Ribolla Gialla
German Riesling
Gruner Veltliner, Kerner

Reds
German Pinot Noir
Lambrusco, Gutturnio
Oltrepò Pavese, Schiava,
Lagrein, Gragnano

LAMB

Rack of Lamb

Reds
Rhône Reds, Pomerol
Brunello di Montalcino
Rosso di Montalcino
Vino Nobile, Barolo
Barbaresco, Aglianico
Uva di Troia, Nero
D'Avola, Washington
State Merlot

Lamb Kebab

Reds
Nemea, Aegean Red
Shiraz, Salice Salentino
Faugères, Nero D'Avola
Zenatta, Syrah
Rhône, Primitivo,
Zinfandel Beqaa Reds

Lamb Chops

Reds
Bordeaux, Priorato
Rioja, Rhône Reds
Nero D'Avola, Shiraz

Lamb Vindaloo

Whites
Riesling, Gruner
Gewurztraminer

Reds
Rioja, Pinot Noir

Spit Roasted Lamb

Reds
Nemea, Salice Salentino
Washington Merlot

Moussaka

Reds
Nemea, Côtes du Rhône
Cannonau, Nero d'Avola

BEEF AND VEAL

Steak

Reds
Bordeaux, Hermitage
Cahors, Madiran, Barolo
Brunello di Montalcino
Taurasi, Pignolo
California Cabernet

Chateaubriand

Reds
Côte-Rôtie
Châteauneuf-du-Pape
Amarone, Refosco
Schiopettino, Australian
Shiraz, Zinfandel

Pot Roast

Reds
Cabernet, Shiraz

Meatloaf

Reds
Cabernet, Shiraz

Chili con Carne

Reds
Côtes du Rhône
Shiraz, Cabernet
Primitivo

Hamburgers

Reds
Shiraz, Cabernet
Zinfandel, Primitivo

Parrillada

Reds
Malbec, Tannat

Ossobuco

Reds
Chianti Riserva
Super Tuscan, Refosco
Barolo, Barbaresco
Valtellina, Gutturnio

Veal Scaloppine "Piccata"/ al Limone

Whites
Tocai Friulano, Ribolla
Gialla, Greco di Tufo

Veal Milanese

Reds
Valtellina, Ripasso
Nebbiolo, Nero d'Avola

Veal Marsala

Whites
Greco di Tufo Soave
Tocai Friulano

Reds
Pinot Noir, Chianti,
Valpolicella, Etna, Nero
d'Avola, Dry Marsala

Bresaola / Carpaccio / Steak Tartare

Reds
Schiava, Oltrepò Pavese
Refosco, Pignolo
Barbaresco, Nebbiolo
Rosso di Montalcino

GAME: Such as Boar Buffalo, Elk, Deer

Reds
Priorato, Valpolicella,
Ripasso, Amarone
Pirmitivo, Aglianico
Brunello di Montalcino

CHEESE

Mozzarella di Bufala and Burrata

Whites
Greco di Tufo
Fiano di Avellino
Falanghina
Campi Flegrei
Coda di Volpe
Ischia Bianco, Ravello
Pallagrello Bianco
Lacryma Christi Bianco

*Goat Cheese such as:
Caprino, Robiola, Montrachet, Boucheron, Chèvre, Crottin de Chavignol*

Whites
Sauvignon Blanc
(Particularly Sancerre)

Rich Double and Triple Cream Cheeses such as Pierre Robert Explorateur Saint André

Champagne
Orange Wines, Oloroso
Sherry, Tokaji Aszù

*Soft Ripened Cheese such as:
Brie, Camembert, Robiola*

Whites
Champagne
Riesling, Gruner

Reds
Pinot Noir, Beaujolais Zweigelt

*Semi Soft Cheese such as
Gouda, Fontina, Emmenthal, Montasio, Crucolo*

Whites
Meursault, Alsace Riesling, Ribolla
Gialla, Tocai Friulano

Semi Hard Cheese such as :
Cheddar, Kasseri, Mahon,
Gruyere, Comte, Bra, Raschera
Primosale, Caciocavallo

Whites
Alsace Riesling, Gewurztraminer,
Gruner Veltliner Alsace Pinot Gris

Reds
Rosso Piceno, Montepulciano d'Abruzzo
Nero d'Avola, Cannonau

Hard Cheese such as :
Parmigiano Reggiano
Grana Padano
Asiago, Piave, Sovrano
Moliterno
Pecorino Crotonese
Fiore Sardo
Roncal
Aged Gouda

Please note :
Parmigiano Reggiano is believed to be the most versatile cheese. It can be matched with nearly every wine and does magnificently well with Champagne.

Sparkling
Champagne, Franciacorta, Proseccoo

Whites
Ribolla Gialla
Tocai Friulano, Riesling, Erbaluce

Reds
Amarone, Ripasso, Barolo, Barbaresco
Nebbiolo d'Alba Brunello di Montalicno
Rosso di Montalcino, Vino Nobile
Super Tuscan, Lambrusco
Châteauneuf-du-Pape

DESSERT

I do not agree with pairing dessert with a sweet wine. The dessert is sweet enough and matching sugary desserts with a sugary drink is just too sugary. The tastes become masked and you cannot appreciate either the dessert or dessert wine. If you must match something with a dessert, try to get a dry wine to cut through the richness of the dessert. The only sweet wines I would probably ever pair with a dessert are Moscato D'Asti or Brachetto d'Acqui, which can actually bring out the flavors of the dessert, but that is only if you must drink a dessert wine with your dessert.

RETAIL

The best, and cheapest, way to discover wines is to buy them from a good wine store. Retail is the most inexpensive and legally possible way of purchasing wine. The only hard part is finding a good wine store, either physical or online. Before addressing the wine shop problem, let's first talk about prices. All wine stores buy from the same people (distributors). Sometimes, if the wine store buys a certain product in bulk, it costs less per case of wine and, therefore, a cheaper price is charged to the consumer.

There are many kinds of stores. You have the mega size stores that are practically wholesalers. They sell the *well-known* brands at cheaper prices, at cost, or sometimes even at a loss. This draws people in and is a great strategy if mass marketed wines are the theme of the store. The problem is that all other less known brands are marked up even higher to help pay for the money lost on the well known products. In short, mega stores offer values only on highly publicized wines that are usually not that great anyway. These mega stores are great if you need to buy a lot of liquor or wines with well known names. The negative, though, is that these stores are not always the place to find unknown wines that do not and cannot charge too high of a price. These wines can be unbelievable values. If the mega store does happen to stock such a wine, it will usually be marked up to an astronomical price. The other downside of mega stores is that you will have a 99% chance of not finding anyone who can really help you and has any knowledge on the subject of wine whatsoever. Most are staffed with college kids trying to make a few extra bucks.

The opposite of the mega store is a smaller, neighborhood store. You are not guaranteed to find great wines in a smaller store, but the probability is much higher than that of a mega store. Small stores operate on smaller budgets and cannot compete with huge stores on prices. This encourages the smart stores to direct their attention to lesser known wines that can be great values at low prices. These prices stay low because the wineries do not pay tons of money for advertising. The small store, if you are lucky, will more likely have a staff that is familiar with the wines and hopefully tastes them all before buying the wines.

A good wine store should have a well informed staff. This includes knowledge of wine and food pairing. The staff should always ask the customer what he or she is eating to better know which wine to offer. If the customer is not having the wine with dinner, the staff member should know which wines are great for situations that do not call for food. The staff member should offer the customer the best wine at whatever price they are willing to spend. A good wine store should also offer a vast selection of non oaked, non mass marketed wines.

As for pricing, the situation does not seem to be getting better. This is usually *not even* the fault of the wine store. Every state has its own liquor laws, but not one stands tall as an example of consumer friendly. New York State, for example, is a miserable place when it comes to liquor laws. They are slowly changing some things around BUT those laws that intrude and increase prices seem to never go away.

Allow me to explain how wine gets from one place to the consumer. Let us take, for example, French wines. Egos and popularity already boost prices, but laws boost them even further. This is not just France; it is every wine country. The wine maker in France is faced with so many stupid laws and taxes that, before it leaves the vineyard, it already costs more than it should. I must not fail to mention that if the winemaker faced a bad year, prices go up to pay for such an occurrence. I'm not just talking about money problems, I am referring to natural problems. If there was a natural disaster, the prices go up.

For an American importer to bring in a wine to this country, that person must first get a license. Of course, there is no need to say that this license comes at a price. Then, when the importer buys the wine, he is paying all kinds of increases from exchange rates and, of course, more taxes on the actual sale. Now, an importer must sell the wine to a distributor who distributes it. An importer can also be a distributor, BUT distributing requires yet another license and yet another fee. Some companies have enough capital and are big enough to take on the distributing side, while others are either not that fortunate or simply do not even bother with the hassle. When an importer sells to a distributor, there is yet another tax imposed. All these taxes and I have yet to discuss the income taxes these people are doomed to face. Now, income tax seems to not really affect the consumer but they do. Most costs end up getting eaten by the customer.

Anyway, I AM NOT FINISHED. The distributor must now sell to restaurants and retailers and, guess what? Another tax is imposed. Now, the retailer and restaurants have to have their own license and that is another fee paid to that good ol' government. When the retailer or restaurant sells the wine to the consumer, there is the final sales tax. In the end, you, the consumer, gets screwed. If this bothers you as a consumer, then I suggest you change your voting habits.

This may shock some people, but the government probably makes more off a bottle of wine or liquor than whoever is involved with the actual making, importing, distributing, and selling of that product. Take, for example, full on socialist countries such as Canada. Canadian wines and liquors actually *cost more in Canada* than they do in the U.S.A.. A Canadian once told me that about 65% of a bottle's cost results from government imposed taxes. Maybe that is not an exact figure, but I would bet it is pretty close. This is absurd. Governments claim to raise taxes on such things as to prevent underage drinking.

COME ON! We know that is a complete joke and so do the government officials who make up these laws. Look at the taxes on cigarettes, for example, called "sin taxes" by moral relativists, of all people! Cigarettes cost $15 a pack in 2019 in NYC. We are told taxing people to death does not discourage economic activity by the same people who tell us they need to raise taxes on cigarettes to discourage smoking? Huh? These taxes in no way prevent people from smoking. Cigarettes aren't my favorite example, as I am disgusted by them, but you get my point. Excessive taxes cut job growth and productivity. That is a "sin".

RESTAURANTS

I am always sympathetic to the cries of businesses when they complain that things cost too much. I believe businesses should be allowed to freely operate with each other to offer the consumer the best price possible. While I understand the need for restaurants to make their money, and they should, I do feel that some simply take it to the next level. Too many restaurants mark up their wines exponentially. In 2019 New York City, I can no longer even blame them. Expenses and costs of doing business are too high. It is now the trend, in New York at least, to mark up a wine 400 – 500 %. The *fair* mark up *used to be* 250 – 300%, but this seems impossible to do and stay in business, sadly.

Of course, the ritzy, incredibly high-end restaurants can justifiably charge high prices for wines. Their clientele can easily afford it. The problem is that not every restaurant is on that level with that clientele. By raising wine prices, the regular restaurants are not changing the reality that their customers *simply do not want to pay such high prices*. This is all being forced on them by hostile, anti-small business governments.

A restaurant should offer wines that go with their food. Too many times, this is unfortunately not the case. The lists offer all these big names that may be good to great but do not compliment their food. These wines are there for purposes of showing off (the whole ego thing). A restaurant that takes wine seriously should have on hand someone who can help the customer choose the best wine that goes with the meal and is in the customer's budget. The restaurant should also offer wines by the glass that not only compliment the food but also hopefully offer the customer a chance at trying something new and exciting.

To the customer, I have only one thing to say. Please do not return a bottle just because it is not what you expected. Once the bottle is opened, you must pay for it. A bottle should only be returned if the wine went bad. The restaurant cannot keep opening wines, at their expense, until you find one you like. I know most people would never do such a thing, but there are those annoying few who feel it is their duty to make others' blood boil.

INDEX

Abruzzo, 94
Acidity, 18, 19, 20
Aegean, 121
Aeration, 20
Ageing, 20
Agiorgitiko, 64
Aglianico, 95
Albariño
    Portugal, 110
    Spain, 116
Albarola, 78
Albana, 80
Alcohol, 18, 20
Aleatico, 92
Alexander Valley, 38
Alfrocheiro, 109
Aloxe Corton, 51
Alsace, 47
Amarone, 87
Anderson Valley, 38
Anjou, 45
Anthocyanins, 20
Appassimento, 20, 80, 87, 88
Appearance, 16
Appellation, 20
Argentina, 31
    La Rioja, 31
    Mendoza, 31
    Patagonia, 31
    Rio Negro, 31
    Salta, 31
Armagnac, 52
Arneis, 75
Aroma, 20
Aromatic, 21
Asprinio, 96
Assyrtiko, 65, 66
Attica, 65
Auslese, 60
Australia, 33
    Barossa Valley, 33
    Coonawarra, 33
    Hunter Valley, 33
    Margaret River, 33
    Yarra Valley, 33
Austria,
    Niederosterreich, 35
Auxey Duresses, 51
Avanà, 77
Avarengo, 77
Avellino, 95
Avola, 99

Baden, 62
Baga, 109
Bairrada, 109
Balance, 19
Bandol, 54
Barbaresco, 76
Barbera, 75-76
Bardolino, 86
Barolo, 76
Barolo Chinato, 77
Barossa Valley, 33
Barrel, 21
Barrique, 21
Basilicata, 97
Basque Country, 118
Bastardo, 109
Beaujolais, 52
Beaumes de Venise, 54
Beerenauslese, 60
Beqaa, 101
Bequet, 77
Bianco di Custoza, 86
Biancolella, 95
Big, 21
Bitterness, 19
Blanc de Morgex et de la Salle, 79
Blaufrankish, 68
Blending, 12, 21
Boca, 76
Body, 18, 21, 123
Bohemia, 42
Bolgheri, 83

Bonarda, 81
Bordeaux, 48-49
Bosco, 78
Botrytis Cinerea, 21
Bouquet, 21
Brachetto D'Acqui, 77
Bramaterra, 77
Breathe, 21
Breganze Torcolato, 88
Bright, 21
Brut, 21
Buttery, 21
Burgundy, 51-52

Cabernet Franc
    France, 45
    Italy, 85
Cabernet Sauvignon
    Argentina, 31
    Australia, 33
    California, 38-39
    Chile, 40
    France, 48, 49, 54
    Hungary, 68
    Israel, 71
    Italy, 83, 85, 92
    Lebanon, 101
    New York, 103
    New Zealand, 105
    Turkey, 121
    Washington, 107
    South Africa, 113
    Spain, 117, 118
Cafayate, 31
Cahors, 52
California, 37-39
    Alexander Valley, 38
    Anderson Valley, 38
    Carneros Valley, 38
    Dry Creek Valley, 38
    Edna Valley, 39
    Mendocino County, 38
    Monterey County, 39
    Napa Valley, 38
    Paso Robles, 39
    Russian River Valley, 38
    Santa Rita, 39
    Santa Ynez, 39
    Sonoma Valley, 38
Calabria, 97
Campania, 95-96
Campi Flegrei, 95
Canaiolo, 82, 83
Cannonau, 100
Carema, 77
Carignan
    France, 55
    Lebanon, 101
    Morocco, 102
    Spain, 116
Carménère, 40
Carmignano, 83
Carricante, 99
Casavecchia, 96
Cassis, 22
Castel del Monte, 98
Catalonia, 117
Catarratto, 99
Cava, 117
Cayuga Lake, 103
Cedar, 22
Centesimino, 81
Central Otago, 105
Cerasuolo d'Abruzzo, 94
Cerasuolo di Vittoria, 99
Cesanese, 92
Chablis, 51
Champagne, 46
Charbono, 81
Chardonnay
    Australia, 33
    California, 38, 39
    France, 46, 51-52
    Israel, 71
    Italy, 79
    Lebanon, 101
    New York, 103
    New Zealand, 105
    South Africa, 113
    Spain, 117
    Turkey, 121

Charmat-Martinetti, 11, 87
Chassagne Montrachet, 51
Chasselas, 120
Châteauneuf-du-Pape, 54
Chatus, 77
Chenin Blanc
    France, 45
    South Africa, 113
Chewy, 22
Chianti, 81
Chile, 40
    Maipo Valley, 40
    Colchagua, 40
Chinon, 45
Christ, 70
Cilento, 96
Cirò Bianco, 97
Cirò Rosato 97
Cirò Rosso, 97
Clarity, 17
Classico, 22, 82
Clean, 22
Closed, 22
Cococciola, 94
Coda di Volpe, 95, 96
Cognac, 50
Colares, 111
Colchagua, 40
Color Hue, 16
Color Intensity, 16-17
Colli Piacentini, 81
Commandaria, 65
Condrieu, 53
Constantia, 113
Coonawarra, 33
Corbieres, 55
Corked, 22
Cornalin, 120
Cornas, 54
Corsica, 56
Cortese, 75
Corvina, 86-87
Coteaux d'Aix en Provence, 54
Coteaux de l'Atlas, 102
Côte Chalonnaise, 51
Côte de Beaune, 51

Côte de Nuits, 51
Côte D'Or, 51
Côtes du Rhône, 53
Côte Rôtie, 53
Crap, 22
Cremant D' Alsace, 47
Croatia, 41
    Dalmatia, 41
    Kontinentalna, 41
    Istria, 41
    Primorska, 41
    Slavonia, 41
Croatina 80, 81
Crisp, 22
Critics, 15
Crozes – Hermitage, 54
Cyprus, 65
Czechoslovakia, 42
Czech Republic, 42
    Bohemia, 42
    Moravia, 42

Dalmatia, 41
Dao, 109
Deep, 22
Delicate, 22
Demi-Sec, 22
Dessert Wine, 28
Dolceacqua, 78
Dolcetto, 75, 78
Douro, 109-110
Doux, 22
Dry Creek Valley, 38
Dryness, 18

Earthy, 21
Edna Valley, 39
Eger, 68
Egri Bikavér, 68
Eiswein, 60
Elegant, 22
Emilia Romagna, 80-81
Enantio, 90
Erbaluce, 75

Etna Bianco, 99
Etna Rosso, 99
Eucalyptus, 22

Falanghina, 95
Falerno del Massico, 96
Famoso, 80
Faro, 99
Faugères, 55
Favorita, 75
Fermentation, 22-23
Foglia Tonda, 83
Fiano di Avellino, 95
Fiano Minutolo, 98
Filtering, 23
Finesse, 23
Finger Lakes, 103
Finish, 19, 23
Firm, 23
Flabby, 23
Flat, 23
Fleshy, 23
Flint, 23
Floral, 23
Forastera, 95
Fortified Wine, 23
France,
   Alsace, 47
      Cremant D'Alsace, 47
   Armagnac, 52
   Bordeaux, 48, 49
     Graves, 49
     Médoc, 48-49
     Margaux, 48
     Pauillac, 48
     Saint Etsèphe, 49
     Saint Julien, 49
     Pomerol, 48
     Saint Emilion, 48
     Sauternes, 49
   Burgundy, 51-52
     Aloxe Croton, 51
     Auxey Duresses, 51
     Beaujolais, 52
     Chablis, 51
     Chassagne Montrachet, 51
     Côte Chalonnaise, 51
     Côte de Beaune, 51
     Côte de Nuits, 51
     Côte D' Or, 51
     Gevrey-Chambertin, 51
     Mâconnais, 52
     Mâcon Villages, 52
     Meursault, 51
     Nuits Saint George, 51
     Pommard, 51
     Pouilly Fuissé, 52
     Puligny-Montrachet, 51
     Saint Véran, 52
     Savigny-Lès Beaune, 51
     Volnay, 51
     Vougeout, 51
     Vosne-Romanée, 51
   Cahors, 52
   Champagne, 46
   Cognac, 50
   Languedoc – Roussillon, 55
     Corbières, 55
     Faugères, 55
     Fitou, 55
     Minervois, 55
     Pinet, 55
     Saint Chinian, 55
     Rivesaltes, 55
   Loire, 45
     Anjou, 45
     Chinon, 45
     Muscadet, 45
     Pouilly Fumé, 45
     Sancerre, 45
     Vouvray, 45
   Madiran, 52
   Provence, 54
     Bandol, 54
     Coteaux d' Aix en Provence, 54
   Rhône, 53-54
     Châteauneuf-du-Pape, 54
     Condrieu, 53
     Cornas, 54
     Côte Rôtie, 53
     Côtes du Rhône, 53

Crozes Hermitage, 54
Gigondas, 54
Hermitage, 53
Tavel, 54
Vacqueyras, 54
Venise, 54
Franciacorta, 79
Franken, 62
Frappato, 99
Frascati, 92
Freisa, 77
Fresh, 23
Friuli Venezia Giulia, 84
Frizzante, 23
Fruity, 23
Fumin, 79
Furmint, 68

Gaglioppo, 97
Galil (Galilee), 70-71
Gamay, 45, 52
Gamey, 23
Garganega, 86
Georgia, 57
    Kakheti, 57
Gattinara, 76
Gavi, 75
Germany, 58-62
    Auslese, 60
    Baden, 62
    Beerenauslese, 60
    Eiswein, 60
    Franken, 62
    Halbtrocken, 61
    Kabinett, 60
    Mosel, 61
    Nahe, 61
    Rheingau, 62
    Rheinhessen, 62
    Rheinpfalz, 62
    Rhine, 61
    Ruwer, 61
    Spatlese, 60
    Saar, 61
    Trocken, 61
    Trockenbeerenauslese, 60
Gevrey-Chambertin, 51
Gewürztraminer
    Austria, 35
    France, 47
    Germany, 62
Gigondas, 54
Gisborne, 105
Glera, 87
Godello, 116
Golan Heights, 70
Gragnano, 96
Grapes, 9
Grapey, 23
Grappa, 88
Grasevina, 41
Grassy, 23
Graves, 49
Grechetto Bianco, 93
Grechetto Rosso, 92
Greco Bianco, 97
Greco di Tufo, 95
Greco di Bianco, 97
Greco Nero, 97
Greece, 63-66
    Attica, 65
    Commandaria, 65
    Cyprus, 65
    Macedonia, 65
    Mantinia, 64
    Metaxa, 66
    Naoussa, 65
    Nemea, 64
    Patras, 64
    Peloponesse, 64
    Retsina, 65
    Samos, 66
    Santorini, 66
    Vino Santo, 66
Green, 24
Grenache
    Australia, 33
    France, 53, 54, 55
    Lebanon, 101
    Morocco, 102
    Spain, 116

    Turkey, 121
Grenache Blanc, 53
Grignolino, 77
Grillo, 99
Grip, 24
Grumello, 80
Gruner Veltliner, 35
Gutturnio, 81

Halbtrocken, 61
Hamptons, 103
Hawke's Bay, 105
Herbaceous, 24
Hermitage, 53
Hondarrabi Beltza, 118
Hondarrabi Zuri, 118
Honeyed, 24
Hudson River Region, 103
Hungary, 68
    Eger, 68
    Nagy Somló, 68
    Tokaj, 68
    Villány, 68
Hunter Valley, 33

Ice Wine, 60
Incrocio Manzoni, 86
Inferno, 80
Inky, 24
Inzolia, 99
Ischia, 95
Israel, 69-71
    Galil (Galilee), 70-71
    Golan Heights, 70-71
    Samson, 71
    Shomron, 71
    Judean Hills, 71
    Lower Galilee, 70-71
    Negev, 71
    Upper Galilee, 70-71
Istria, 41
Italy, 72-100
    Abruzzo, 94
    Basilicata, 97

    Vulture, 97
Calabria, 97
    Bianco, 97
    Cirò, 97
Campania, 95-96
    Avellino, 95
    Campi Flegrei, 95
    Cilento, 96
    Gragnano, 96
    Ischia, 95
    Massico, 96
    Ravello, 95-96
    Taurasi, 96
    Tufo, 95
    Vesuvio, 96
Emilia Romagna, 80-81
    Gutturnio, 81
Friuli Venezia Giulia, 84-85
Lazio, 92
    Frascati, 92
Liguria, 78
    Dolceacqua, 78
    Sciacchetrà, 78
Lombardia, 79-80
    Franciacorta, 79
    Grumello, 79
    Inferno, 79
    Oltrepò Pavese, 80
    Sassella, 79
    Valgella, 79
    Valtellina, 80
Marche, 91
    Morro D'Alba 91
    Rosso Conero, 91
    Rosso Piceno, 91
Molise, 94
Piemonte, 75-77
    Barbaresco, 76
    Barolo, 76
    Bramaterra, 77
    Boca, 76
    Carema, 77
    Gattinara, 76
    Gavi, 75
    Lessona, 76
    Pinerolese Ramìe, 77

Puglia, 98
   Castel Del Monte 98
   Locorotondo, 98
   Manduria, 98
   Salice Salentino, 98
Sardegna, 100
   Oristano, 100
Sicilia, 99-100
   Avola, 99
   Etna, 99
   Faro, 99
   Lipari, 100
   Marsala, 100
   Pantelleria, 100
   Vittoria, 99
Toscana, 82-83
   Bolgheri, 83
   Carmignano, 83
   Chianti, 82
   Montalcino, 82
   Montepulciano, 82
   Scansano, 83
Trentino Alto Adige, 89-90
Umbria, 93
   Montefalco, 93
   Orvieto, 93
Valle D'Aosta, 79
   Blanc de Morgex et de la Salle, 79
Veneto, 86-88
   Bardolino, 86
   Custoza, 86
   Grappa, 88
   Lessini Durello 87
   Lugana, 86
   Recioto della Valpolicella, 88
   Recioto di Gambellara, 88
   Recioto di Soave, 88
   Soave, 86
   Valpolicella, 86

Jammy, 24
Jarbola, 41
Jerez, 118
Jesus Christ, 70
Judean Hills, 71

Jumilla, 118

Kabinett, 60
Kakheti, 57
Kékfrankos, 68
Kerner, 89
Kontinentalna, 41
Kosher, 70
Kvevri, 57

Lacrima di Morro D'Alba, 91
Lacryma Christi del Vesuvio Bianco, 96
Lacryma Christi del Vesuvio Rosso, 96
Lagrein, 89
Lambrusco, 80-81
Lamezia Terme, 97
Languedoc Roussillon, 55
La Rioja, 31
Lazio, 92
Leathery, 24
Lebanon, 101
      Beqaa, 101
Lessini Durello, 87
Lessona, 76
Lettere, 96
Liguria, 78
Lipari, 100
Lively, 24
Location, 8
Locorotondo, 98
Loire, 45
Lower Galilee, 70
Lombardia, 79-80
Long Island, 103
Lugana, 86
Lush, 24

Macabeo, 117
Macedonia, 65
Maceration, 24
Mâconnais, 52
Mâcon Villages, 52
Madeira, 111
Madiran, 52

Magliocco Canino, 97
Magliocco Dolce, 97
Maipo Valley, 40
Malbec
    Argentina, 31
    France, 52
Malolactic Fermenation, 24
Malvasia, 84, 100
Malvazija, 41
Mammolo, 56
Manduria, 98
Mantinia, 64
Marche, 91
Margaret River, 33
Margaux, 48
Maremma, 83
Marlborough, 105
Marmara, 121
Marsala, 100
Marsanne, 53
Martinborough, 105
Marzemino, 90
Matching Wine and Food, 123
Mature, 24
Mavro, 65
Mavrodaphne, 64
Meaty, 24
Médoc, 48-49
Meknès, 102
Melon de Bourgogne, 45
Mendocino County, 38
Mendoza, 31
Menu, 124-135
Merlot
    Australia, 32
    Chile, 40
    California, 38
    France, 48-49
    Italy, 85, 92
    Washington, 107
    South Africa, 113
    Spain, 117
    Switzerland, 120
Merwah, 101
Metaxa, 66
Meursault, 51

Mevushal, 70
Minervois, 55
Minty, 24
Molar, 111
Molinara, 86-87
Molise, 94
Monastrell, 118
Monica, 100
Moravia, 42
Morocco, 102
    Coteaux de l'Atlas, 102
    Meknès, 102
    Northen Plain, 102
    Zenatta, 102
Moscophilero, 64
Mosel, 61
Montalcino, 82
Montefalco, 93
Montepulciano (grape), 94
Montepulciano (town), 82
Monterey County, 39
Montonico, 97
Morellino di Scansano, 83
Moscato, 77, 100
Moscato Giallo, 89
Moscato Rosa, 90
Mourvèdre
    France, 53, 54, 55
    Israel, 71
    Spain, 118
Muller Thurgau, 42, 62
Muscadelle, 49
Muscadet, 45
Muscat
    Greece, 64
    Italy, 78, 89, 90, 100
Muscat de Beaumes de Venise, 54

Nagy Somló, 68
Nahe, 61
Naoussa, 65
Napa Valley, 38
Navarra, 116
Nebbiolo, 76, 77, 79, 80
Negev, 71

Negra Mole, 111
Negrara, 146
Negroamaro, 98
Nemea, 64
Nerello Cappuccio, 97, 99
Nerello Mascalese, 97, 99
Nero D'Avola, 99, 100
New World Wines, 12
New York, 103
    Cayuga Lake, 103
    Hamptons, 103
    Hudson River Region, 103
    Long Island, 103
    North Fork, 103
New Zealand, 105
    Central Otago, 105
    Gisborne, 105
    Hawke's Bay, 105
    Marlborough, 105
    Martinborough, 105
Niederosterreich, 35
Nielluccio, 56
Noble, 21, 24, 82
Noble Rot, 24
Nocera, 99
North Fork, 103
Nosiola, 89, 90
Nuits Saint George, 51
Nuragus, 100
Nutty, 25

Oak, 25
Obaideh, 101
Off, 25
Off Dry, 25
Olivella Nera, 96
Oltrepò Pavese, 79, 80
Open, 25
Orange Wine, 11, 28, 57, 80
Oregon, 107
    Williamette Valley, 107
Oristano, 100
Ormeasco, 78
Orturgo, 81
Orvieto, 93

Overripe, 25
Oxidized, 25
Paarl, 113
Pallagrello Bianco, 96
Pallagrello Rosso, 96
Palomino, 116
Pantelleria, 100
Parellada, 117
Passerina, 91
Paso Robles, 39
Passito di Sagrantino, 93
Patagonia, 31
Patras, 64
Pauillac, 48
Pecorino, 94
Pelaverga, 77
Peloponnese, 64
Penèdes, 117
Periquita, 109
Pessac-Léognan, 49
Pétillant Naturel, 11
Petit Arvine, 79
Petit Rouge, 79
Petit Verdot, 48, 49
Piedirosso, 95, 96
Picolit, 85
Picotendro, 79
Picpoul de Pinet, 55
Piemonte, 75-77
Pigato, 78
Pignoletto, 80
Pignolo, 85
Pinorelese Ramìe, 77
Pinotage, 113
Pinot Bianco, 89
Pinot Blanc, 47
Pinot Grigio, 84, 89
Pinot Gris, 47
Pinot Noir
    Australia, 33
    California, 39
    France, 51
    Germany, 62
    Italy, 79
    New York, 103
    New Zealand, 105

    Oregon, 107
    Switzerland, 120
Pinot Meunier
    France, 46
    Italy, 79
Plavac Mali, 41
Pomace, 25
Pomerol, 48
Pommard, 51
Port, 110-111
Portugal, 108-111
    Bairrada, 109
    Colares, 111
    Dao, 109
    Douro, 109-110
    Madeira, 111
    Port, 110-111
    Vinho Verde, 110
Pouilly Fuissé, 52
Pouilly Fumé, 45
Posavska, 112
Posip, 41
Podravska, 112
Powerful, 25
Preto, 109
Prié Blanc, 79
Primitivo, 98
Primorska,
    Croatia, 41
    Slovenia, 112
Priorato, 117
Prosecco, 87
Provence, 54
Prugnolo, 82
Puglia, 98
Pugnitello, 83
Puligny-Montrachet, 51

Raisiny, 25
Ramisco, 111
Rasteau, 53
Ravello, 95-96
Rebo, 90
Rebula, 112
Recioto della Valpolicella, 87, 88

Recioto di Gambellara, 88
Recioto di Soave, 88
Red Wine, 9-10
Refosco, 85
Refosk, 41
Residual Sugar, 25
Restaurant, 138
Retail, 136-137
Retsina, 65
Rheingau, 62
Rheinhessen, 62
Rheinpfalz, 62
Rhine, 61
Rhône, 53
Rias Biaxas, 116
Ribera del Duero, 116
Ribeiro, 116
Ribolla Gialla, 84
Ribolla Nera, 85
Rich, 25
Riesling
    Austria, 35
    California, 39
    France, 47
    Germany, 60-62
    Italy, 79, 84
    New York, 103
Rioja, 116
Rio Negro, 31
Ripasso, 87
Ripe, 25
Rivaner, 42
Rivesaltes, 55
Rkatsiteli, 57
Roditis, 65
Rondinella, 86, 87
Rosato 26
Rosé, 10, 26
    France, 45, 46, 54, 56
    Greece, 65
    Italy, 86, 94, 97
    Spain, 116
Rossese, 78
Rosso Conero, 91
Rosso Piceno, 91
Rough, 26

Round, 26
Roussanne, 53
Rueda, 117
Russian River Valley, 38
Ruchè, 77
Ruwer, 61

Saar, 61
Saint Chinian, 55
Saint Emilion, 48
Saint Estèphe, 49
Saint Julien, 49
Saint Laurent, 42
Saint Véran, 52
Sagrantino, 93
Salice Salentino, 98
Salta, 31
Samos, 66
Samson, 71
Sancerre, 45
Sangiovese, 78, 81, 82, 83, 91, 93
Sangue di Giuda, 80
San Lunardo, 95
San Nicola, 96
Santa Rita, 39
Santa Ynez, 39
Santorini, 66
Saperavi, 57
Sardegna, 100
Sassella, 80
Sauvignon Blanc
    France, 45, 49
    New Zealand, 105
    South Africa, 113
    Spain, 117
Savatiano, 65
Savigny-Lès Beaune, 51
Savuto, 97
Scavigna, 97
Schiava, 90
Schioppettino, 85
Scheurebe, 62
Sciacarello, 56
Sciacchetrà, 78
Sciascinoso, 96

Second Label, 26
Sediment, 26
Serving Wine, 28
Semillon
    Australia, 33
    France, 49
    Lebanon, 101
Sforzato, 80
Sfurzat, 80
Shiraz
    Austria, 33
    France, 53, 54, 55
    Italy, 92
    Morocco, 102
    South Africa, 113
Shomron, 71
Sicily, 99-100
Slavonia, 41
Smell, 17
Smoky, 26
Soave, 86
Sonoma Valley, 38
South Africa
    Constantia, 113
    Paarl, 113
    Stellenbosch, 113
    Swartland, 113
Spanna, 76
Spain, 114-118
    Catalonia, 117
    Cava, 117
    Jerez, 118
    Jumilla, 118
    Navarra, 116
    Penèdes, 117
    Priorato, 117
    Rias Biaxas, 116
    Ribera del Duero, 116
    Ribeiro, 116
    Rioja, 116
    Rueda, 117
Sparkling Wine, 11
Spatlese, 60
Spicy, 26
Spumante, 26
Steely, 26

Storing Wine, 28
Structure, 26
Susumaniello, 98
Sweetness, 18
Sweet Wine, 11
Sylvaner, 62
Syria, 70
    Golan Heights, 70
Syrupy, 27
Switzerland, 120

Tannat,
    France, 52
    Uruguay, 122
Tannins, 18, 19, 27
Tar, 27
Tart, 27
Taste, 17
Tasting Wine, 16-19
Taurasi, 96
Tavel, 54
Tazzelenghe, 85
Tempranillo
    Spain, 116
    Portugal, 110
Teroldego, 89
Terran, 41
Terrano, 85
Terroir, 27
Texture, 27
Thick, 27
Timorasso, 75
Tinta Barocca, 110
Tinta Cao, 110
Tinta Pinheira, 109
Tinta Roriz, 110
Toasty, 27
Tobacco, 27
Tocai Friulano, 84
Tokaj, 68
Tokaji D'Aszù, 68
Torbato, 100
Torrontés, 31
Touriga Francesa, 110
Touriga Nacional, 109, 110

Toscana, 82-83
Traditional Method, 11
Traminer, 89
Trebbiano, 82, 83, 92, 94
Trebbiano di Lugana, 86, 88
Trentino Alto Adige, 89-90
Trocken, 61
Trockenbeerenauslese, 60
Tufo, 95
Turkey, 121
    Aegean, 121
    Marmara, 121
Txakoli, 118

Ugni Blanc, 50
Umbria, 93
Unfiltered, 27
Underripe, 27
Upper Galilee, 70
Uruguay, 122
    Canelones, 122
Uva di Troia, 98
Uva Rara, 81

Vacqueyras, 54
Valgella, 80
Valle D' Aosta, 79
Valpolicella, 86
Valtellina, 80
Vanilla, 27
Varietal, 27
Vegetal, 27
Veneto, 86-87
Verdeca, 96, 98
Verdelho, 110
Verdicchio, 91
Verduzzo, 85
Vermentino, 82, 100
Vernaccia di Oristano, 100
Vernaccia di San Gimignano, 82
Vernaccia Nera, 91
Vespaiola, 86
Vespolina, 76
Villány, 68

Vinho Verde, 110
Vin Santo, 83
Vino Santo, 66
Vines, 8-9
Vineyard, 8-9
Vintage, 27
Viognier, 53
Vitovska, 84
Vittoria, 99
Volnay, 51
Vougeout, 51
Vouvray, 45
Vulture, 97

Washington State,
    Walla Walla Valley, 107
    Yakima Valley, 107
Watery, 27
Weather, 8
Welschriesling, 41
White Wine, 10
Winemaking, 8-10
Winery, 9-10
Wine Tasting, 16-19
Wine Terms, 20-27

Xynomavro, 65
Xarel-lo, 117

Yarra Valley, 33
Yakima Valley, 107

Zenatta, 102
Zibibbo, 100
Zinfandel
    California, 38
Zweigelt, 35

www.ingramcontent.com/pod-product-compliance
Lightning Source LLC
Chambersburg PA
CBHW081155290426
44108CB00018B/2560